The Promise of the Father

The Baptism in the Holy Spirit

Dr Nikolas Howarth MB BCh MA

Life Publications

Acknowledgments

I have had so much help and advice in preparing this book that it would be impossible to mention everyone individually. I am particularly grateful to those who have read and re-read the script, both in part and in whole. Their comments have been invaluable. The book started out as Bible study notes for the Wednesday house group, which was particularly rich in wisdom and maturity. They were the trigger for causing me to turn the notes into a book. Their patience for my excesses, encouragements during my messes, corrections of my errors, probing questions and honesty in letting me know when I was incomprehensible, were the anvil on which this book was forged. Finally, my sincere gratitude to my co-minister and his wife Paul and Lynne Wood, who, together, have proof read and proof read, encouraged, prayed and kept me focused. Thank you all.

E–Mail: nik@nikolashowarth.com
www.nikolashowarth.com

Cover design by Graham Alder, the cover picture is taken from the mosaic by Einar Forseth in the Chapel of Unity, Coventry Cathedral.

First Published October 2008, by Life Publications, Merthyr Tydfil, South Wales, UK.

Dedication

To my wife, Maggie

Contents

Part 1
The Olive Tree
An Exegetical Study

Part 2
The Traveller
A Metaphysical Study

Introduction

If I lived in the desert and had never seen snow I may believe that, in England, it always snows at Christmas as that is what I have been taught and observed on millions of Christmas cards. If, by some good fortune, I were to one day find myself in London on December 25th and note that it was not snowing and was not likely to snow, then I may hold rigidly to my belief that it is not Christmas, because it is not snowing, and it always snows at Christmas!

When our expectation and our observations do not tie up it can be difficult to go with the observations and much easier to stay with the belief given by our expectation or tradition. This is not a book on economics, but someone once said to me that there was only one cause of bankruptcy – not believing the figures. On reflection, I doubt that that is true. I expect that we believe the figures, yet somehow get into a frame of mind in which we do not expect them to matter and we hope that they will change.

I have an elderly friend to whom the word “Geranium” means a particular plant. The fact that that is not the name of that plant is neither here nor there for her, what she means is “Pelargonium”. It is difficult for her to change and is of little consequence to her, until she starts trying to order plants from the nursery.

The term "the Baptism in the Spirit" is a phrase to which most Christians have attached a meaning. Notwithstanding the fact that different denominational groups have clear teaching on what this means to them there is no widely agreed understanding. The questions that are asked usually reflect the view held by the questioner. What I mean is that when I am asked by someone to give my opinion on the nature of the "initial evidence" I have to assume that the questioner has already decided that the Baptism in the Spirit refers to a single event after salvation. I am left rather like a man looking at a green apple and being asked whether it is pink or blue.

This book seeks to set out a theology of the Baptism in the Spirit. One of the biggest obstacles to doing this is in the language. When I use the phrase "Baptism in the Holy Spirit" those who are listening immediately think that I am referring to what they mean by that phrase, when, in fact, I may be referring to something entirely different.

Summary

What I mean by the Baptism in the Spirit is as follows. As the Holy Spirit is an individual, any interaction with this individual, the third person of the trinity, must take place in the context of a relationship. This Baptism is the process by which a sinner is turned into a soldier. It starts when the sinner is first convicted by the Holy Spirit and starts to respond. It finishes when that individual has received spiritual gifts and is using them for God's service. The Baptism in the Spirit, by this definition, is not subsequent to, or part of salvation. Rather, salvation is part of the process of the Baptism in the Spirit. It has three stages, conviction, salvation and equipping. The details of these three stages with their gifts and final ministries are unique to each individual.

This book sets out the reasons for this belief.

Prologue

This book is in two parts. The first part, called *The Olive Tree*, is an exegetical exploration of the Baptism in the Holy Spirit. The second part, *The Traveller*, looks at the same subject but in a very different way, its approach is more metaphysical.

I first started to write this book some 35 years ago, although the book that I have written now is very different to the book that I would have written then. As a young doctor, I had spread my time evenly between the various Christian Unions and student groups of the hospitals and University that surrounded me, and my church, the Cardiff City Temple, which was lead by P.S. Brewster who was my first Pastor.

The Temple, under P.S. (as we all affectionately knew him, which is a very un-British way of addressing anyone) was a strong moderate Pentecostal fellowship in which I felt very comfortable. Its Welshness showed in its worship and the warmth of its people; its moderation showed in its orderliness and structure; its outreach showed in its vision and life; and its balance showed in its doctrine. It became for me a model on which I would and will always compare my own models of "church".

I was equally at home in the various Hospital Christian Groups, which were conservative evangelical, reformed, and academic. This was the early 1970s, before the charismatic movement in the UK and the development of the house group movement. My problem was that although I was perfectly comfortable in these two environments, many of those within them felt uncomfortable with me; they seemed to feel that I should make up my mind and choose between them. I never did. The leading to write this book, and its title, came from that time. I did sit down and start to write it then. However, it did not take long before I understood God to be saying, "Write it, yes, but not now! You will know when the time has come to start it."

Now I am a leader of a small English church and I can say that I never did choose between the two. Neither has the church that I am privileged to lead, in fact those within it would hardly see a conflict, and neither do I. There are, and until Jesus returns, always will be areas of difference within the community of those who know and follow Christ. Nevertheless, none of us is perfect and none of us yet has it all right. I have learnt to live with the differences and enjoy the concordances.

The idea of writing down my thoughts on the Baptism in the Spirit stayed in my mind, simmering away. I knew that one day I would come to write them down, but, as age tends to make you less impatient with time despite the fact that you have less of it, I was not in any hurry to enter into the project: God is not in a hurry.

Shortly after the Christmas service in 2003, as I was leaving the church, I became engaged in a conversation with our newly formed Wednesday Bible study group – what should we do next? We had just finished Ephesians and I had suggested that the group decide over Christmas what they would like to do in the New Year. The suggestion was that we looked at the work of the Holy Spirit. That was the request, specifically, that we looked at what it means to be Baptised in the Spirit.

I produced and gave out each week's Bible study notes. Little by little, I began to notice that the book was forming itself. Each weekly study notes provided the material for one chapter. (At the price of some repetition, I have endeavoured to keep that structure, each chapter being suitable for a group Bible study.) Some individuals however, persisted in asking me the question, "What *happens* when the Spirit changes us?" It was in trying to answer this question (my co-pastor's wife being particularly persistent in her questioning) that *The Traveller* was born. After some months of exegetical study, the Wednesday Bible group became the workshop for exploring *The Traveller*, each chapter being a week's study. This exposed us to a very different style of study, which not all found easy but some seemed to revel in! (My wife, a member of this group, much preferred *The Olive Tree*.)

The Traveller does plug gaps and opens areas that *The Olive Tree* does not. Both works approach the same subject but from very different angles. *The Traveller's* approach is one that is speculative and metaphysical and I do not want to appear to give more of an authority to it than speculation allows; there is, here, plenty of room for discussion and room to dissent. Its role is to clarify some of the issues that arise from *The Olive Tree,* notably, what *happens* to us when we are baptised in the Spirit.

Part 1

The Olive Tree

An exegetical approach to the Baptism of the Holy Spirit

Chapter 1

This is Important

"The man on whom you see the Spirit come down and remain is He who will baptise with the Holy Spirit."
John 1:33

* The Baptism in the Holy Spirit is important
* Statements about the Baptism in the Holy Spirit mark the beginning and end of Jesus' ministry
* There are different views as to what this means
* This book seeks to understand what God meant when he told us that Jesus would Baptise us in the Holy Spirit

The essential meaning of "Christian" is that it describes one who follows Christ. If he leads my life and my thoughts, his teachings and sayings must be the light by which I see all else. Predominantly, we find his teaching in the four Gospels. Certainly, his teaching radiates throughout the whole Bible but it is in the four Gospels that he speaks most clearly. If we wish to understand him, then we will do no better than to start our exploration in these Gospels, where we can measure all else by what he says, does and shows.

All Scripture is God-breathed and useful for teaching, rebuking, correcting and training in righteousness, so that the godly may be thoroughly equipped for every good work.[1] Throughout this book, I use scripture from all parts of the Bible with equal authority and weight but all scripture needs interpreting and the way to interpret scripture is by scripture. The Gospels and the words of Jesus are the brightest beams by which to do so.[2]

The Holy Spirit did not present these Gospels haphazardly. Jesus' words are not careless expressions; they are teaching from the heart of God. Those who wrote the Gospels did not just sit down and throw some past thoughts, memories, and experiences into a pot. They carefully, under the Holy Spirit's guidance, wrote down and reflected the mind of God. We must pay great attention to what is said, the way in which it is said, and where and when it is said, for not one thought is a chance, God intends it all.

There is great significance in the way that Jesus ministry is introduced. God intends Jesus' first reported words to herald his ministry and to open up our understanding to his teaching. Jesus' last reported words are meant to summarise his intentions and to lead the church into the church age. What are these first and last words? We cannot find the actual Aramaic words; we are seeking God's introductory thoughts.[3] I am seeking to look to God and to

---

[1] 2 Timothy 3:16-17.

[2] Luke 24:45.

ask, "In the written sermons that record the life of Jesus, what was your first point and what was your last?" – and every preacher knows that those are significant points.

God told John the Baptist to tell us that Jesus will baptise with the Holy Spirit. All four Gospels start the same way, with this declaration – Jesus will baptise with the Holy Spirit. Surely, this is significant and important.

Matthew, Mark and Luke are called the synoptic gospels; "synoptic" is Greek for "from the same view". In other words, they all approach the life of Jesus in a very similar way but each makes significant and unique points.

Each of these Gospels starts differently. Matthew with Jesus' lineage, Mark gets straight into Jesus' ministry, and Luke gives us the stories of Jesus' birth.

In Matthew, after he has given us an introduction, we are led to the story of John the Baptist. John, the greatest of all the prophets, has the role of announcing Jesus to the world. He announces that Jesus

---

[3] God gave us the New Testament in the ancient Greek language that is called *Koine* Greek or New Testament Greek. *Koine* means common. It was the common language of the Eastern Mediterranean at the time of Christ and for hundreds of years before and after. It has great similarities to the Classical ancient Greek used by poets such as Homer and little similarity to the Modern Greek spoken today. Koine Greek is not spoken today. Jesus spoke his words in Aramaic, which were translated into Koine Greek by the Gospel writers. This was deliberate; it is what God intended. Why so, is an interesting question. Maybe part of the reason is to demonstrate that the Word of God belongs to all cultures and to show that to be understood it must be interpreted. The Gospels tell us in Koine Greek of events that occurred to people speaking in Aramaic. Our Gospels are translations from Koine Greek into our own languages; the original Aramaic spoken words are hidden with God. In this book, when it says "Greek", it means New Testament Koine Greek.

will baptise his followers with the Holy Spirit. This is the herald's call.

When we look at Mark, we find exactly the same thing. John announced Jesus to the world as the one who will Baptise in the Holy Spirit.

And Luke? After his detailed account of Jesus' birth, he also leads us to John the Baptist. Luke picks up on the same theme, Jesus, he says, will Baptise in the Holy Spirit.

All three synoptics start the same way. John the Baptist announces Jesus public ministry to the world. The announcement is that Jesus will Baptise in the Holy Spirit.[4]

> **All four Gospels say that Jesus' ministry was introduced to the world by John the Baptist declaring that "Jesus shall Baptise in the Holy Spirit."**
>
> **This must be important.**

The Gospel of John is written from an entirely different view from the three synoptics and has little in common with them, but even here we see a remarkable consistency. John's Gospel starts with the wonderful description of the nature of Jesus. Then he leads us rapidly into a picture of John the Baptist in Judea. You can almost hear and feel the words and ministry of John in this wonderful graphic passage. We are taken into John the Baptist's teaching and declaration as the Gospel writer builds up the expectation in our minds: who is John and who is Jesus? Finally, John brings us to the

---

[4] Matthew 3:11; Mark 1:8; Luke 3:16.

climax of his statements and the passage closes after making this powerful declaration.

> *"I would not have known him, except that the one who sent me to baptise with water told me, 'The man on whom you see the Spirit come down and remain is he who will baptise with the Holy Spirit.' I have seen and I testify that this is the Son of God,"* John 1:33-34.

This is how the Gospels start. This is the introduction to Jesus. The one who was born of the lineage of David, who came to this earth through miraculous birth, who is the very essence of God, being one with God, through whom all things were made and created, this one, Jesus, came to us to baptise us with the Holy Spirit: that's why he came, that's why he was sent.

How do the Gospels end? Matthew does not end with great detail. The Gospel says that the remaining eleven disciples went to the mountain where Jesus had told them to go. This clearly implies that Jesus knew what he was going to do and had previously prepared the disciples. On the mountain, despite some doubting from the disciples, he commissioned them to take his news to the peoples of the earth.[5] The promise that he will be with them always indicates that his leaving was not absolute.[6]

Mark shares the same points but in differing contexts. It appears from Mark that Jesus commissioned the disciples on more than one occasion; it appears that the commissioning words may have been given in locations other than the mountain. That is not surprising or

[5] Matthew 28:16-20.

[6] A point that we can clearly understand: he left on the mountain, but he has appeared since (for example: Paul on the Damascus Road and John in Revelation) and he will return again.

inconsistent because Jesus often repeated his messages.[7] But Mark adds to our picture by saying that Jesus was "taken up" to heaven.[8]

The Gospel of John finishes by the lake with Jesus talking with the disciples. Immediately before this, John has recorded some of the events surrounding the appearances of the risen Lord.

John 20:20-22

> *"After he said this, he showed them his hands and side. The disciples were overjoyed when they saw the Lord. Again Jesus said, 'Peace be with you! As the Father has sent me, I am sending you.' And with that he breathed on them and said, 'Receive the Holy Spirit.'"*

Luke gives us two accounts, one in his Gospel and one at the start of Acts. His Gospel is consistent with Matthew and Mark. We can glean that Jesus led them to the mountain in Bethany. Here, whilst he was blessing them he was taken up to heaven. The commission had been given before (as Mark says) but must have been repeated on the mountain (as Matthew says). They are told to stay in the city until they receive what the Father had promised, which is linked to the receiving of power.[9]

At the end of his earthly ministry, Jesus taught that the disciples must wait for the Baptism with the Holy Spirit.

---

[7] For example, the Lord's Prayer appears to have been given twice in two different locations, during the Sermon on the Mount and after a period of prayer. Matthew 6 and Luke 11.

[8] Mark 16.

[9] Luke 24:45-53.

In Acts, Luke tells us more. After the resurrection, Jesus appeared to them for forty days, teaching them about the kingdom of God.[10] The statement that they were to wait until they received the gift that the Father had promised was given to them whilst they were all assembled together, possibly for a meal. It was not a one-off statement but it was part of something that Jesus had regularly taught. The gift that the Father promised is the Baptism in the Holy Spirit.

Acts 1:4-5

> *"On one occasion, while he was eating with them, he gave them this command: 'Do not leave Jerusalem, but wait for the gift my Father promised, which you have heard me speak about. For John baptised with water, but in a few days you will be baptised with the Holy Spirit.'"*

Here we have a clear insight into the nature of the power that was to come; it is power to witness and carry out the commission.

Acts 1:7-8

> *"He said to them: 'It is not for you to know the times or dates the Father has set by his own authority. But you will receive power when the Holy Spirit comes on you; and you will be my witnesses in Jerusalem, and in all Judea and Samaria, and to the ends of the earth.'"*

After giving this teaching, Jesus was taken up from them.[11]

---

[10] Acts 1:3.

[11] Acts 1. He was taken up from off the mountain but the teaching may have been given elsewhere.

Now we have a clear picture of the end of Jesus public earthly ministry. After his resurrection, he appeared to and taught the disciples, his family, and others. We do not know all the points that he taught but the Gospel writers give us at least two.

Firstly, the believers were to take the news of Jesus and his teachings into the whole world. Secondly, they were to wait until they had received the power to do this. This power, that Jesus said was promised by the Father, is Holy Spirit Baptism.

Statements about Spirit Baptism mark the beginning and end of Jesus' ministry.

God meant this.

It is important.

The idea of Spirit Baptism both opens and closes the ministry of Jesus. This is not an accident; this is God's design.

These are points that we cannot ignore. Jesus ministry starts with the idea of the Baptism in the Spirit and ends with the idea of the Baptism in the Spirit. God could hardly have given a greater prominence to this teaching and it is unthinkable that it should be incomprehensible but today there is confusion. Some believe that this promised gift refers to one single event after salvation, others that it is only a way of describing salvation.

Spirit Baptism is important but today it is the subject of a great deal of confusion and disagreement.

A good friend of mine once said to me that what we Christians lacked was an ability to see that what we do not understand may have been given to others; all we have to do is to be humble enough to listen. In other words, we should approach others with the attitude of "What has God told this person that he has not told me?"[12]

This book seeks to understand what God meant when he told us that Jesus would Baptise us in the Holy Spirit.

This book seeks to understand what God meant when he told us that Jesus would Baptise us in the Holy Spirit.

[12] This is a reflection by Dr. Noel Greenhalgh, which he made to me after repeatedly falling off his sailboard whilst being unable to put into practice exactly what the instructor was saying.

Chapter 2

The Lord is One

"Hear, O Israel: The LORD our God, the Lord is one."
Deuteronomy 6:4

* God is one
* But God is in three persons
* Those three persons can be seen in the Old Testament
* To understand who the Holy Spirit is we have to understand who God is
* This chapter helps us understand how the Holy Spirit, who is a person, is part of the divine trinity

The nature of God is simple. God is one. If we are to understand anything of a concept that is described as a baptism into the deity, we must have an understanding of the nature of God. There is only one creator God and God is one.

Yet Christians have fallen out over this concept and it has caused division and difficulty. The reason for these difficulties is the problem in grasping that although God is one he presents himself to us as more than singular. This book is not a study of ontology but we must at least consider this issue.[13] As we do so, let us remind ourselves of the difficulties; God is one, yet not singular. This has been accepted as essential Christian doctrine since the 4th century, being considered at Nicaea in 325 from which we have the Nicene Creed. After this, for about 700 years, the Church debated and reconsidered the issues; the divinity and separate personalities of the Father, Jesus and the Spirit were (and still are) accepted without question, as they should be. What was in question was the relationship between them, their ontology. One thousand years ago, the church divided over this ontology.[14] The divide was not over the trinity but the ontology of the trinity: they agreed that there was a trinity but disagreed about the nature of the relationships within that trinity. Since Nicaea in 325, the divinity of the Father, Son and Spirit

[13] "Ontology" is a classical Greek word much loved by philosophers and theologians. It names an area of metaphysics concerned with the essence of things, what they are and how they relate to each other. In theological terms "ontology" is usually used when considering the nature of the essence of God, particularly the trinity.

[14] The Nicene Creed was agreed in 325. In 589 a clause was added that altered the ontological understanding. The Latin speaking churches proposed and accepted this change. The Greek speaking Churches did not. The disagreement lasted until 1054 when the church divided into the Greek based Eastern Orthodox Church and the Latin based Western Roman Church. The ontology of the trinity was one of the given reasons for the divide but conflicts over power, influence, language and patronage may also have been involved. We must be careful not to do the same. It would be uncharitable to infer that some of our present doctrinal dispositions are influenced by concerns of power, influence, language, history, tradition and patronage rather than understanding alone.

and their separate personalities was never in question, the divide was over the relationship between the personalities of the trinity. When you think about it, it is incredulous that the church should divide over such an issue. Who could be so certain that, from the position of mere humanity, one could claim to know the essence of God so accurately, and being so confident as to the depth of the others' error, as to break fellowship, labelling the others as heretics and taking up violent arms against them?[15] It is and always has been healthy, and indeed essential, for there to be dialogue, debate and discussion amongst Christians. Such considerations should add to our understanding and our fellowship. When they lead to a breaking of fellowship over issues that are not essential to salvation then one would do well to consider whether other issues and agendas are also at work.[16]

There is only one creator God and God is one.

The trinity, that God is three in one, is essential and clear enough, but to argue and insist on exact word formulas to describe that union, to me, is pretentious. God is at peace with himself; there is no jealousy or tension between the persons of the trinity. And how could there be for God is one. To allow human division over the demonstration of the perfect harmony that is the trinity is to be defeated. To resort to violence and abuse is to have walked away from Christ's calling and example.

---

[15] This sin continues right up to today, the sin of claiming to do God's work with violence.

[16] Agendas like power and patronage. Jesus said that we should know one another by our love not our theology.

God is at peace with himself.

God is one, in three persons.

God is one, yet in three persons. He exists in perfect unity and harmony. If we need to stress anything it is his oneness and his harmony. The apostle Paul reminds us that we see such things obscurely as if through frosted glass; we see the shadows of truth, we do not yet see all truth itself.[17] Let us remind ourselves of that; that our doctrine, especially in these areas, is an approximation of the whole glory that is God and we should hold it in careful humility. We should not hold it in doubt, but with a recognition that others may see it slightly differently than we do.[18]

God hints at his plurality from the opening pages of the scripture. He says *"Let us make man in our image, according to our likeness"*.[19] Is God describing himself as "us" or is he addressing others in the heavenly host? If he is addressing a heavenly host he is asking them to be part of the creating, which we know is not possible for God is the only creator. There seems to be only one

---

[17] 1 Corinthians 13:12. Paul may be referring to a looking glass that was not perfect so it distorted the image.

[18] If we *believe* we are right and others are wrong, then let us thank God for what he has shown us, giving him the thanks and glory, not attributing any such insights to our own abilities. Even if we do have such great abilities, God gave them. So in all things it is God who is glorified and not ourselves.
"Be generous with the different things God gave you, passing them around so all get in on it: if words, let it be God's words; if help, let it be God's hearty help. That way, God's bright presence will be evident in everything through Jesus, and he'll get all the credit as the One mighty in everything — encores to the end of time. Oh, yes!" 1 Peter 4:9-11 (from THE MESSAGE: The Bible in Contemporary Language © 2002 by Eugene H. Peterson. All rights reserved.)

[19] Genesis 1:26

coherent view of this passage, God is describing himself in the plural.

In Genesis 32:24-30 Jacob wrestled with a man. Jacob asked and insisted that the man bless him. The man did. Jacob's name and life was changed from that moment on. He was no longer "Jacob" but "Israel" because he had struggled with God (v.28). Jacob described the event by saying that he had seen God face to face. We can find other examples in the Old Testament of a man who appears and is accorded the honour due to God.[20]

The Old Testament also contains a Presence that is not a person with a body, but who is the manifestation of God. The Angel, or Messenger, of the Lord appeared to Moses in the burning bush. It is clear that this is God himself. God appeared to Israel over the Tabernacle in the form of a pillar of fire by night and cloud by day. Cloud and fire enveloped Mount Sinai when Moses was given the Ten Commandments. Hundreds of years later when Solomon prayed for the sanctifying of the Temple, the Temple was filled with a cloud so dense that because of the glory of the Lord the Priests ministering there could not continue with their duties.[21] This presence of God is often called the Shekinah presence, from the Hebrew meaning "dwelling place". [22]

---

[20] Compare Josh. 5:13-15 with Rev. 19:10 and 22:9 for example.

[21] Exodus 13:21; 24:16-18; 40:34-38; Num. 9:16-18; 2 Chron. 5:13-14. Also Rev.14-14; Some would attempt to argue that this is not evidence of a third person of the trinity but just evidence of the presence of the person of God. I cannot accept this for reasons that are apparent in the New Testament. This is discussed in the next chapter.

[22] Chapter 3

We can see in the Old Testament a picture of God who has three persons.

- **There is the God of Heaven.**
- **There are examples of a being who has a body and is recognised as a man.**
- **There is a presence that is often manifest in fire and cloud.**

We can see in the Old Testament a picture of God who has three persons. There is the God of Heaven. There are examples of a being who has a body and is recognised as a man. There is a presence that is often manifest in fire and cloud. These are all God, and are not separate for God is one. But they are also distinct. The God in bodily form appears to strengthen and counsel. The Shekinah presence appears to be closely associated with God's dwelling.[23]

It is not difficult for Christians to see the Father, Son, and Holy Spirit in these passages. That God is one is a clear statement of scripture. That he is three in one is not difficult to see.[24] It is important for Christians to understand and reflect upon the oneness of God just as much as on the three persons.

I once had our youth group make a tetrahedron. This is the object that has the smallest number of flat sides, four; you cannot make anything out of less than four flat sides. It is like a three-sided pyramid. What they did was to make it so as it did not have a base

---

[23] Mount Sinai was the dwelling place of God. God moved his dwelling to the Tabernacle. Later he moved it to the Temple.

[24] There are many scriptures that lead us to this view. I have use these few to introduce the scriptural base for the trinity.

but was held together by the other three sides. On one side we put the word "Father"; on another the word "Son"; and on the third we put the words "Holy Spirit". You can then place it on its (missing) base and you have a three-sided pyramid. The side that you are looking at declares "Father", "Son", or "Spirit". If you pick it up and look at the missing base what you see is the underside of the other three sides. On one under-side we wrote "G", on the other "O" and on the last "D". This tetrahedron is one object with three parts, each side is separate but each makes up the whole. But God is more than that. We cannot explain or demonstrate God completely by a tetrahedron or a leaf but such examples are helpful to us.[25]

It is important for Christians to understand and reflect upon the oneness of God just as much as on the three persons.

The picture we have from the Old Testament is of one God. He is the creator God. God's desire is to be in fellowship with his creation. He gave his creation over to the government of humanity. His desire is to bring humanity into accord with him.

God is one, but in three persons. God is always present; we use the term "omnipresent" to describe this attribute. We use the term "manifest presence" to describe times and places where God reveals himself as a discernable presence, in a time and space.[26] The person

---

[25] St Patrick famously compared the trinity to a shamrock leaf.

[26] There may have been many bushes apparent to Moses as he observed the burning bush. God was no less present in a non-burning bush than he was present in the burning bush. God made his presence clear to Moses through the burning bush in a way that registered with Moses senses, including his sight. Our senses are considered a little more in Part Two – The Traveller, particularly in chapter one.

of the Holy Spirit was manifest with the Shekinah. The Shekinah was the seal of the dwelling place of God. In Solomon's reign the Shekinah moved to the Temple. Hundreds of years after that, due to the sins of the Jewish people God moved his dwelling back to Heaven.[27] Israel was conquered by a foreign nation and taken into captivity. The Spirit of God was taken from the Temple.

Ezekiel 10:18

> *"Then the glory of the LORD departed from over the threshold of the temple and stopped above the cherubim."*

The Old Testament closes with God's dwelling removed from the earth, with God and mankind estranged. The Holy Spirit was removed from the Temple, the very dwelling place of God.

The Old Testament closes with separation – but promises hope.

But it does not end there. The prophets bring the promise of God's restoration. God, they said, will give a way back. His dwelling will be with men. The Old Testament ends with the hope of restoration and the New opens with a promise.

That promise is that he will not only return the Shekinah, that he will not just restore his dwelling upon the earth, but that he will dwell with us and so immerse those who follow him in his presence

[27] The story of Israel from the prophets onwards shows us that this was not lightly done. God removed the Shekinah only after centuries of gross sins that included human sacrifice.

that they may constantly live as his glory. This return of the Spirit is not just a doctrinal consideration, it is more than a single experience – it is a total enveloping, a baptism: the promise of the Father is that he will Baptise us in the Holy Spirit.

Chapter 3

Who is The Holy Spirit?

"Then He said, 'Do not draw near this place. Take your sandals off your feet, for the place where you stand is holy ground.'"
Exodus 3:5 (NKJV)

* There is a Baptism in the Spirit
* This comes from Jesus
* There is a Holy Spirit who is seen in both the Old and New Testaments
* The Holy Spirit is a person, the third member of the trinity

John's Gospel opens with the glorious statement

"In the beginning was the Word, and the Word was with God, and the Word was God," John 1:1. (KJV)

Of the four Gospels, his celebrates the deity of Jesus as the second person of the trinity most clearly. There are many other passages in the Bible that show this to us but in John we find that the picture of Jesus being one with the Father shines from stories and chapters. One of John's purposes in writing his Gospel was to proclaim this truth. To understand this nature of Jesus is an essential part of spiritual growth.

The Christian message is Christocentric. That is to say it is centred on Christ; on his teachings on how we should live, on his provision for our forgiveness and salvation, and on the hope that he gives for our secure eternity. It is an observation that many of the tendencies towards imbalance in some of today's Christian approaches are due to the mistake of allowing the person and teaching of Christ to slip from the centre of focus. In some cases, this is because the teaching has become Pneumocentric, centred on the Holy Spirit.[28] As we shall see one of the jobs of the Holy Spirit is to glorify Jesus. To make the Spirit the centre of our attention is to make his job more difficult as the Spirit's job is to make Christ the centre of our attention. We must be careful to remain Christ centred, that is, Christocentric.[29]

At the start of the four Gospels and at the start of Acts we have the following statement impressed upon us by the Scriptures:

Jesus will Baptise in the Holy Spirit.

---

[28] *Pneuma* in Greek means breath, wind, and Spirit.

[29] It is inevitable that in a book which sets out to look at one of the aspects of the Spirit's ministry the Spirit should become central to those themes. This is not to imply a pneumocentric theology. It is also not acceptable to ignore such teaching in case the teaching becomes pneumocentric. If we took that approach we would not teach on the Father in case that teaching led us away from a Christ centred approach.

Jesus gives this baptism. He is the Baptiser in the Holy Spirit. The Father sent him to baptise in the Spirit.

Without the life, teaching, death and resurrection of Jesus there would not and could not be any such baptism.

That there is such a baptism is clearly proclaimed by scripture. That Jesus is the Baptiser is also clear. That there is a Holy Spirit is clear. But who is he?

Without the life, teaching, death and resurrection of Jesus there would not and could not be a Baptism in the Spirit.

Jesus is the Baptiser in the Holy Spirit.

He is seen in the Shekinah.[30]

We have seen that in the Old Testament there is a presence of God that is linked to his dwelling place and represented by fire and cloud. This presence was taken back to heaven by God and from the Temple during the time of Ezekiel. Just before and maybe at his ascension Jesus told the disciples to go and wait in Jerusalem until power came upon them, power that would aid them in being his witnesses.

Acts 2:1-4

1 When the day of Pentecost came, they were all together in one place.

[30] "Shekinah" is not a word that appears in the scripture, but is a word that is taken from Hebrew to describe this particular manifestation of God. It means "dwelling".

2 Suddenly a sound like the blowing of a violent wind came from heaven and filled the whole house where they were sitting.

3 They saw what seemed to be tongues of fire that separated and came to rest on each of them.

4 All of them were filled with the Holy Spirit and began to speak in other tongues as the Spirit enabled them. (NIV)

This is the Shekinah presence, the same presence that was removed from the Temple. Each Shekinah manifestation in the Old Testament marked a covenant change between God and humanity.

In Exodus 3, the Shekinah presence of God was manifest when God spoke to Moses through the burning bush. We can see that there is some consistency when the Shekinah is manifest and there is clearly a link between the presence of the Shekinah and the unfolding events.

* The place where the Shekinah is manifest is revealed by fire or cloud. Exodus 3:2
* There is a manifest presence of God shown by God calling to Moses, Exodus 3:4
* God ordains the place as holy [31]
* There is a covenant change, Exodus 3:12
* Because of the covenant change God's "dwelling place" changes, Exodus 3:12

[31] Chapter 6 discusses holiness.

* There is an historical continuity, in other words, a moving forward from the present situation, Exodus 3:15

When Moses was on Mount Sinai we see the same properties with the continuing presence of the Shekinah.[32]

The Shekinah was manifest at the dedication of the Tabernacle. All the manifestations of the Shekinah that were present at the burning bush were present at the dedication of the Tabernacle. There was cloud and light. The manifest presence of God came onto the Ark. The Tabernacle became holy. God moved his dwelling place to the Tabernacle. This was part of the historical continuity. [33]

The Law was now established through Moses and the tabernacle had become the centre of worship and the dwelling place of God.

The next change came with the dedication of the Temple. David had collected all the materials to build the Temple, and Solomon built it. When it was dedicated, the Shekinah was manifest. There was a cloud that filled the Temple. The presence of God was such that the priests could not minister for the glory of the Lord had filled the house. The Temple became The Holy Place. Until that moment, Israel had continued to worship God at the Ark. (It would appear that the Tabernacle was no longer in existence.) After the dedication of the Temple, and this manifestation of the Shekinah, the Temple became the replacement for the Tabernacle. Israel was to worship at the Temple that became the permanent home for the Ark. The Temple became the dwelling place of God. This was part of historical continuity.[34]

---

[32] Ex 24:16. Num 9:16-23.

[33] Exodus 40: 8, 34-38.

[34] 1 Kings 8:10-13. 2 Chronicles 5:13.

Due to Israel's disobedience, particularly that of human sacrifice, God allowed them to be taken into captivity and the Temple to be destroyed. The prophet Ezekiel saw the Shekinah being taken back to heaven in a vision.[35] Nevertheless, the story does not end there as he, and the prophet Zechariah, prophetically see the Shekinah return to God's people at a future time.[36]

The day of Pentecost was the return of the Shekinah, now manifest in the New Covenant. God now dwells with his church. The presence was manifest with wind and fire, the tongues of fire settling on each one individually signifying both the individuality of our relationship with God and a corporate identity (Luke 3:16). The powerful presence of God was shown by the speaking in identifiable tongues of different languages, showing that this gift belonged to all (Zechariah 2:11). The church, as a body of believers is called to holiness.[37]

There is covenant change, the New Covenant. Now God is worshiped through Jesus and he dwells in his Church. This is the continuation of the prophetic and historical narrative.

The Holy Spirit is the power in the Shekinah,
He is our Advocate – He led Jesus
He has emotions.

The Holy Spirit is our advocate.

John's Gospel uses the word *parakletos* a number of times to describe the Spirit.[38] This word has a spectrum of meaning that gives

---

[35] Ezekiel 11:23.

[36] Ezekiel 43:2-7. Zech. 2:10-13, 8:3.

[37] See chapter 6.

[38] John 14:16; John 14:26; John 15:26; John 16:7; I John 2:1.

us a clear picture of the Holy Spirit as our advocate. It is used of one who is summoned, called to one's side, especially called to one's aid. It is used of a judge, a pleader or a counsel for defence, a legal assistant, hence "advocate". In the widest sense it is used of a helper, an assistant.[39] John only uses the word *parakletos* to describe the Holy Spirit apart from one occasion where he uses it of Jesus.[40] John compares the coming Holy Spirit directly with Jesus, saying that God will send *"another"* in place of Jesus, the inference clearly being that this "other (*allos*)" was to be the equivalent of the Son.[41]

This concept of an Advocate, a Counsellor, an other, demands a person, not a power.

The Holy Spirit is a person, the third person of the trinity.

The Spirit has emotions as well as personality

Ephesians 4:30
"And do not grieve the Holy Spirit of God, with whom you were sealed for the day of redemption."

Jesus was led by the Spirit

Matthew 4:1
"Then Jesus was led by the Spirit into the desert to be tempted by the devil."

---

[39] Thayer.

[40] In 1John 2:1, John uses the word *parakletos* for Jesus ("one who speaks to the Father in our defence – Jesus Christ, the Righteous One"). Previously his only use of this word was for the Holy Spirit. Is John attributing the same title to both, and thus the same attributes?

[41] John 14:16

Luke 4:1

"Jesus, full of the Holy Spirit, returned from the Jordan and was led by the Spirit in the desert."

The Holy Spirit is a person, the third person of the trinity, who is in a relationship with Jesus.

In all our considerations of the Holy Spirit, we need to keep this foremost in our thinking, that is, the understanding that we are talking about a person, who is the third member of the trinity. If we consider any human engagement with the Spirit, *we are talking about a relationship*. We consider our relationship with the Father and our relationship with the Son so we must see our engagement with the Spirit as a relationship and not a dispensation. To be involved, in any capacity, with a person defines a relationship, an interaction between individuals. The nature of a relationship between two human beings will clearly be different from that of a relationship between the divine creator God and his created being, but it is a relationship and defined as one by God.

We must be careful to consider the significance of this. The Holy Spirit is a person with whom we may enter into a relationship. Relationships are processes that take time and develop over time. A first meeting may be very significant and memorable but a meeting does not make a relationship. We are not invited to just meet the Spirit, but to know the Spirit.[42] We must consider all contacts with the Spirit as part of a relationship.

---

[42] Romans 8:9-10.

Chapter 4

Baptisms

"Remain in me, and I will remain in you. No branch can bear fruit by itself; it must remain in the vine. Neither can you bear fruit unless you remain in me."
John 14:4

- * The meaning of words in the phrase "The Baptism with the Holy Spirit"
- * The meaning of "with"
- * The spectrum of uses in the New Testament of the word "baptism"

What does "with" mean?

We have already noted that God gave us the New Testament in Greek and that Greek and English do not always exactly coincide.[43] This is true of the little word "with"

[43] See chapter 1 footnote 3. This is an easy point for linguists to grasp but may not always be for the rest of us. We could make an analogy with some of our local

as used in the phrase "Baptism with the Holy Spirit". If we are to understand what "Baptism" means we need to be clear about the exact meaning here. The word that we translate "with," is the Greek word *en*, which is one of those words that is not easy to translate into English as a simple single short word. The English word "with" implies the idea of being alongside, or accompanying but independent.

The Greek word for "with" is *en*. It is not easy to translate into English with a simple short word.

If I walk with someone, they are walking alongside me. If I play a musical instrument with others, we are playing together. *En* means more than that; "with" is not involving enough. For this reason, *en* is often translated as "in". This does not help too much either. "In" indicates the idea of enclosure, containment or envelopment; you can be in a box, in a cave, in a good mood, or in an orchestra. This is too controlling and restricting for *en*.

English phrases. My wife is not from the same national group as I am; she is Welsh and I am English, but she is a native English speaker. When we were first married, we began to notice differences in our language that could (potentially) cause some problems. One was the phrase "quite nice". Where she came from to say something was "quite nice" meant that it was almost nice, but not quite. Where I came from it meant that it was especially nice. In our early relationship, I could not work out why she seemed upset after she had prepared something for me and I had gone out of my way to tell her that it really had been "quite nice". There are bound to be such examples in the translation of any language into another; words do not have exactly similar meanings. A well known example of this is the English word "love" which commonly translates both the Greek words *philos* and *agape*, loosing their distinctive meanings. God gave us those two words in the Scripture and he meant something by that. Occasionally it can be helpful to translate accordingly, even if it makes the English a little less elegant.

Helpfully, in John 15:1-4, there is an excellent picture of what *en* means.[44]

1 *"I am the true vine, and my Father is the gardener.*

2 *He cuts off every branch* ***in*** *me that bears no fruit, while every branch that does bear fruit he prunes so that it will be even more fruitful.*

3 *You are already clean because of the word I have spoken to you.*

4 *Remain* ***in*** *me, and I will remain* ***in*** *you. No branch can bear fruit by itself; it must remain in the vine. Neither can you bear fruit unless you remain in me."*

In this passage the word "**in**" is the translation given of *en*. The picture that we have is *"No branch can bear fruit by itself; it must remain* ***in*** *the vine."*

Now the branch is not "in" the vine in the sense of "in" a box; it is plainly outside of the vine. If the branch were "in" the vine then its leaves would be in the vine and in the dark! Furthermore, it would be impossible to prune the branches from the vine without destroying the vine. Neither is it "with" the vine. It is not dissociated and independent.

---

[44] I am not suggesting that this is the only way that *en* is used but I am suggesting that it is coherent to understand *en* in this way. This passage from John gives us a clear picture of its use in the phrase "The Baptism in (*en*) the Spirit".

> **The picture that we have is "No branch can bear fruit by itself; it must remain in (*en*) the vine."**
>
> **The branch is "part of" the vine. It is closely associated to the extent of union with the vine.**
>
> **Here is independence that is interdependent.**

The branch is "part of" the vine. It is closely associated to the extent of union with the vine. Whereas one end of the branch is in the vine, it then emerges from the vine making the other end free, blowing about in the wind, catching rays and making grapes. The branch has a separate identity yet is completely dependent upon the vine for its support and existence. The word *en* describes such a relationship. The branch is both in and with the vine: it is separate, yet part of the whole. It is independent in that it is responsible for fruit bearing, yet it cannot bear fruit by itself.

And this is how Jesus asks us to be. We are to remain *en* him and he will remain *en* us. If we fail to do this we will be fruitless. The fruit that we are created to bear is only possible within (or *en*) this relationship. Here there is independence that is interdependent: we are the branches and he is the vine.

> **This is the relationship that is described by the word *en*. The branch is both in and with the vine: it is separate, yet part of the whole. It is independent in that it is responsible for fruit bearing, yet it cannot bear fruit by itself.**

What does the idea of "Baptism" mean?

If we take a small poll of Christians and ask them "What is Baptism?" I think that we will nearly always get a reply that relates to an initiation rite involving water.[45] Different denominations do this differently but all involve water and all see it as an initiation into the Christian Church.[46] In the Bible, the concept of "Baptism" is much wider than this. If we are to understand what the phrase "Baptised *en* the Spirit" means, we will need to explore the full meaning of the word "baptise".

Jews before John the Baptist used water baptism as an initiation into Judaism.[47] The word "baptism" comes from the Greek word that means, "to dip" but the word has much wider use than that! In the New Testament, it has many uses.

---

[45] Indeed, when I looked into a popular Bible dictionary I found that the only reference was to water baptism! IVF 1970. Try such a poll yourself; just ask a dozen Christians what they think of when you use the word "baptism".

[46] Some baptise infants by anointing with water; others only baptise confessing adults by total immersion. I have no comment to make on this issue in this book. I would reflect that the archaeology of churches dating back to the 2nd century in the Middle East might give us a useful idea of what happened in the primitive and maybe apostolic church.

[47] This is not disputed historically. There is some debate as to where the rite came from and its nature. Jewish law provided for the use of water in ritual cleansing (see Leviticus 11:25, 40; 15:5-7); and Elisha commanded the Syrian commander Naaman to dip himself in the Jordan River to be cleansed of leprosy (see 2 Kings 5). Well before John the Baptist, converts to Judaism were required to bathe (or baptise) themselves as a sign of entering the covenant. Some of the later prophets envisaged that Jewish exiles returning home would cross the Jordan and be sprinkled with its water to cleanse them of sins prior to the establishment of the kingdom of God (see Ezekiel 36:25). In this tradition John the Baptist urged Jews to be baptised in the Jordan for the remission of sins.

There are two Greek words that mean being put into something, *baptizo* and *bapto*. Let us look at *bapto* first. In the following verses *bapto* is used and is translated as dip.

Luke 16:24

> *"So he called to him, 'Father Abraham, have pity on me and send Lazarus to dip the tip of his finger in water and cool my tongue, because I am in agony in this fire.'"*

John 13:26

> *"Jesus answered, 'It is the one to whom I will give this piece of bread when I have dipped it in the dish.' Then, dipping the piece of bread, he gave it to Judas Iscariot, son of Simon."*

Revelation 19:13

> *"He is dressed in a robe dipped in blood, and his name is the Word of God."*

The word *baptizo* has a wide range of uses.

If our understanding of Baptism were only about dipping then the Greek writers would have used the word *bapto*, but they used *baptizo*, which means that they must imply something more.[48]

---

[48] It would be quite reasonable to disagree with this point by suggesting that the two words are almost synonymous, like "swill" and "rinse", only defined by context. This would not alter my overall case; that if "*baptizo*" has a wide meaning, it is acceptable to apply it to the idea of a process.

It is the word given to describe the Baptism of John the Baptist. John administered this baptism in recognition of the baptisand's commitment to a new life. He only gave this water rite to those who first asked for it. We should not ignore this. Clearly, the baptisand needed a change of heart and this change of heart was integral to the process. The water rite was part of a stream of events; recognition, repentance, requesting, submitting and washing, the whole process was the Baptism.

The Church uses the word "Baptism" to describe water initiation and it is easy to see this as an event rather than a process. However, we need to ask ourselves what we mean by the word "event". Every Christian Baptism / initiation rite takes place within a context. With infant baptism, the context is the Church, the family and a liturgy with a Celebrant. With adult believers baptism the context is the confession of the individual and the acceptance of that confession by the Church expressed in a liturgy, which is the baptismal service. The water rite alone is not Baptism; it is only significant within the process that makes up the whole.[49] In every Baptism tradition, the water rite is part of the series of events that constitute the whole process, the whole process is the Baptism. To say that Baptism is a single event is to over simply.

Jesus described his whole ministry as *baptizo* and told James and John that they would be baptised in the same baptism. Jesus described himself as distressed until this baptism was completed.

[49] If the water rite alone was sufficient, non-believers could be effectively baptised, or, in the case of infants, infants who are clearly outside of the Church could be baptised. This is not the case. The "event" of the water takes place within a series of events which are part of the context. This is a process, by which I mean, a series of events. The idea of a journey is helpful, as when Israel left Egypt.

Christ is talking about his ministry, which included distress and martyrdom, a baptism of suffering. [50]

The point that I am making is that the use of the word baptism implies a process that results in change.

The word used for Jewish ceremonial cleansing was *baptizo*.[51] The word *bapto* is not used. Such ritual washing was part of Jewish worship signifying cleansing and belonging. It was a process of

---

[50] In both Mark10:38-39 and Luke12:50 the verb "baptise" occurs in the aorist tense. As English does not have an aorist tense, this is not easy to translate. This tense gives an action, but does not give a corresponding time in which the action occurs. English nouns are like this. If I say "cat" I am referring to a cat, I am giving no indication as to where the cat is in time. In Greek if I say "jump" in the aorist, I am referring to the action of jumping, I am not saying when the jumping takes place. If we indicate the aorist tense as {a}an English translation of Luke 12:50 would be, "I have a baptism <u>baptise{a}[with]</u>, and how I am distressed until it is accomplished!" To make sense of this in English it could be translated as either, "I have a baptism <u>to be baptised with</u>, and how I am distressed until it is accomplished!" or "I have a baptism <u>with which I am being baptised</u>, and how I am distressed until it is accomplished!" (Plainly, this is not a past action or the distress would be over.) Both are equally accurate (or inaccurate, depending on how you would like to see it). In Luke 12:50 the Greek neither proves nor disproves the concept that this baptism of Jesus was ongoing with his ministry. I believe that the context of this verse, taken with Mark 10:38-39 strongly supports the idea that this is an ongoing baptism and Luke 12:50 is better translated as, "I have a baptism <u>with which I am being baptised</u> and how I am distressed until it is accomplished!" Mark 10:38-39, "You don't know what you are asking," Jesus said. "Can you drink the cup I drink or be baptised with the baptism I am baptised with?" "We can," they answered. Jesus said to them, "You will drink the cup I drink and be baptised with the baptism I am baptised with," (NIV).

[51] Mark 7:4, Luke 11:38. In these verses *baptizo* is translated by the verb "to wash."

change, after the washing the worshiper was in a different spiritual state than before.

Paul describes the Jewish nation as being baptised (*baptizo*) into Moses in the cloud and in the sea when they left Egypt and entered the promise land.[52] The crossing of the sea marked the leaving of Egypt and, as we have seen in the earlier chapter, the cloud is the representation of the Holy Spirit. This is a baptism of leaving and joining, leaving Egypt and joining with the presence of God. It was a long process, a journey. Some may say that the Baptism was an event that took place at the crossing of the sea. If we propose this then we are back trying to define an event. Crossing the sea was a long and difficult process. "Event" or "process" matters little; these are just loose definitions of time. It was a journey from one physical place to another and a journey from one spiritual place to another.

"Baptise" is a translation of the Greek word *baptizo*. This word is used in a wide context.

It carries the idea of permanent change following a process. We can see it as a journey from one spiritual place to another.

At the time of writing the Gospels, the word *baptizo* had been in common use for hundreds of years. It appears that its uses and meanings were quite wide. To us today the word "baptise" tends to have only one meaning being our Christian initiation rite. To John the Baptist's listeners this was not so.

I am making the following points:

---

[52] 1 Corinthians 10:2.

- * The "event" of the water initiation is part of a stream of events. It is the whole process that is baptism
- * The world *baptizo* has a wide and uncertain number of meanings [53]
- * It is easy to accept that *baptizo* may be used to describe a spiritual journey that moves from one spiritual state to another
- * We can understand the references to Israel's Baptism *"in the cloud and the sea"* as a journey that starts in one spiritual state and ends in another (I Corinthians 10:2)

---

[53] John the Baptist almost certainly never used the word *baptizo*, and probably neither did Jesus. They spoke Aramaic. God has given us the scripture in Greek. Whatever John said, when he introduced Jesus to the world as the one who would baptise in the Holy Spirit, is lost to us. We can only be certain of what the Gospel writers give us, and they give us the Greek word *baptizo.* This was a deliberate choice of wording, led by the Holy Spirit. Scholars and linguists may be able to propose the Aramaic that was used. Such an exercise may be helpful to our understanding but this is still a backward extrapolation from the Greek and it is only the Greek text that is authoritative. There have been many years of examination of the meaning of *baptizo* by Greek scholars. It has been suggested that *bapto* is always used in a literal sense and *baptizo* in a cultic sense. Others have suggested that in the New Testament *baptizo* has three distinct senses: a theological sense, an initiatory sense and an experiential sense. I remain unconvinced because there is a danger here of the theology defining the use of the word, and then the use of the word being used to define the theology. What is safe is to recognise that: this Greek word was chosen by the gospel writers to convey meaning to the listeners of John the Baptist; that it has a wider spectrum of use than just applying to the moment of water initiation; that hundreds of years of scholarly investigation have not given us a precise meaning.

* We can understand the Baptism that Christ underwent as a process that started with one spiritual state and ended in another (Mark 10:38-39, Luke 12:50) [54]

Those who were baptized by John would have seen his baptism as a fuller and more complete way of ceremonial washing. John clearly identifies the water baptism that he gave with the baptism that Christ was to give "*en* the Holy Spirit". John's baptism was a baptism of repentance, closely linked with the idea of the forgiveness of sin and of purification.

We could attempt to paraphrase what John was saying like this.

I, John, use water to Baptise you following your repentance. This is only to prepare you for the one who is coming. He will take you and change you through the Holy Spirit. God will change you into new, lasting and different spiritual beings. He, yes he, the one that comes, will provide for this journey, a journey that takes you from where you are now to a place of being *en* the Holy Spirit.

In the way that the branch is in the vine, so you will be in the Spirit.

---

[54] It starts with the human race lost in sin and ends with the provision of salvation.

Chapter 5

What is Meant by "Holy"?

"But just as he who called you is holy,
so be holy in all you do."
1 Peter 1:15

* The meaning of the word "holy"; it means things and places that are set apart for God
* Jesus considers attitudes to be holy as well as things
* Holiness is demanded by God
* We must make an effort to be holy

From the very beginning of the Bible we are introduced to the idea of something being "holy".

Genesis 2:3

"And God blessed the seventh day and made it holy, because on it he rested from all the work of creating that he had done."

Exodus 3:1-5

> *"Now Moses was tending the flock of Jethro his father-in-law, the priest of Midian, and he led the flock to the far side of the desert and came to Horeb, the mountain of God.*
>
> *There the angel of the LORD appeared to him in flames of fire from within a bush. Moses saw that though the bush was on fire it did not burn up.*
>
> *So Moses thought, 'I will go over and see this strange sight – why the bush does not burn up.'*
>
> *When the LORD saw that he had gone over to look, God called to him from within the bush, 'Moses! Moses!' And Moses said, 'Here I am.'*
>
> *'Do not come any closer,' God said. 'Take off your sandals, for the place where you are standing is holy ground.'"*

The Hebrew word for "holy" is *qodesh* and means apartness, holiness, sacredness, separateness. It is used of God, of places and of things.[55]

Wherever the Shekinah was became "holy" it was set apart for God.

We can follow this effect of the Spirit through the building of the Tabernacle starting in Exodus 26.

Similarly in 2 Chronicles chapter 5 we see that it is the coming of the Shekinah that shows God's acceptance of the new Temple.

In the Old Testament "Holy" meant a place or a thing that was set apart for God.

[55] The Sabbath would be considered as an institution. *Qodesh* is rarely used of abstract ideas.

Jesus, in answering a point raised by the Pharisees, tells them that the gold of the Temple is made holy (i.e., set apart for worship only) by the authority of the Temple (Matthew 23:16 ff). The Temple is made holy by the presence of the Spirit. We can see that there is a consistent principle, that the place where the Spirit is becomes holy. The idea of the "Holy" Spirit is more than just a description of the Spirit. In other words, it is saying that holiness is an attribute of the Spirit, where the Spirit is must become holy: it must be set apart for God. Or, because the Spirit is there, it *has* been set apart by God.

In the New Testament the Spirit is also introduced to us with the accompanying idea of holy (Matt. 1:18). The Greek word is *hagios* (hag'-ee-os) from *hagos* sacred (physically pure, morally blameless or religious, ceremonially, consecrated).

But whereas in the Old Testament, under the law, holiness was seen as something or some place set apart for God Jesus revolutionises the teaching to include not just places but attitudes which can be both holy and unholy.

In the following passage he teaches us what is not holy.

Mark 7:1-5

> *"The Pharisees and some of the teachers of the law who had come from Jerusalem gathered around Jesus and saw some of his disciples eating food with hands that were 'unclean,' that is, unwashed. (The Pharisees and all the Jews do not eat unless they give their hands a ceremonial washing, holding to the tradition of the elders. When they come from the marketplace they do not eat unless they wash. And they observe many other traditions, such as the washing of cups, pitchers and*

kettles.) So the Pharisees and teachers of the law asked Jesus, 'Why don't your disciples live according to the tradition of the elders instead of eating their food with 'unclean' hands?'"

Mark 7:14-23

"Again Jesus called the crowd to him and said, 'Listen to me, everyone, and understand this. Nothing outside a man can make him 'unclean' by going into him. Rather, it is what comes out of a man that makes him 'unclean.'"

After he had left the crowd and entered the house, his disciples asked him about this parable. 'Are you so dull?' he asked. 'Don't you see that nothing that enters a man from the outside can make him 'unclean'? For it doesn't go into his heart but into his stomach, and then out of his body.' (In saying this, Jesus declared all foods 'clean.')

He went on: 'What comes out of a man is what makes him 'unclean.' For from within, out of men's hearts, come evil thoughts, sexual immorality, theft, murder, adultery, greed, malice, deceit, lewdness, envy, slander, arrogance and folly. All these evils come from inside and make a man 'unclean.'"

Jesus shows us that attitudes can be holy and unholy. Attitudes can be set apart for God, holy, and pleasing to him or they can be offensive to God.

The Greek word for "unclean" is *koinos* (koy-nos') which means shared by all or several, or ceremonially profane, ordinary, belonging to generality, unhallowed, profane, Levitically unclean. In other words it is the opposite of holy.

Paul elaborates further.

Philippians 4:8

> *"Finally, brothers, whatever is true, whatever is noble, whatever is right, whatever is pure, whatever is lovely, whatever is admirable – if anything is excellent or praiseworthy – think about such things."*

Romans 12:1-2

> *"Therefore, I urge you, brothers, in view of God's mercy, to offer your bodies as living sacrifices, holy and pleasing to God – this is your spiritual act of worship. Do not conform any longer to the pattern of this world, but be transformed by the renewing of your mind. Then you will be able to test and approve what God's will is – his good, pleasing and perfect will."*

And Peter also:

1 Peter 1:15-17

> *"But just as he who called you is holy, so be holy in all you do; for it is written: 'Be holy, because I am holy.' Since you call on a Father who judges each man's work impartially, live your lives as strangers here in reverent fear."*

1 Peter 2:1

> *"Therefore, rid yourselves of all malice and all deceit, hypocrisy, envy, and slander of every kind."* (NIV)

We can look at Paul's description of the fruit of the Spirit in the lives of believers.

Galatians 5:16-26

> *"So I say, live by the Spirit, and you will not gratify the desires of the sinful nature. For the sinful nature desires what is contrary to the Spirit, and the Spirit what is contrary to the sinful nature. They are in conflict with each other, so that you do not do what you want. But if you are led by the Spirit, you are not under law.*
>
> *The acts of the sinful nature are obvious: sexual immorality, impurity and debauchery; idolatry and witchcraft; hatred, discord, jealousy, fits of rage, selfish ambition, dissensions, factions and envy; drunkenness, orgies, and the like. I warn you, as I did before, that those who live like this will not inherit the kingdom of God.*
>
> *But the fruit of the Spirit is love, joy, peace, patience, kindness, goodness, faithfulness, gentleness and self-control. Against such things there is no law.*
>
> *Those who belong to Christ Jesus have crucified the sinful nature with its passions and desires.*
>
> *Since we live by the Spirit, let us keep in step with the Spirit. Let us not become conceited, provoking and envying each other."*

In the New Testament holiness is clearly an internal quality. It is a condition of our hearts. We are exalted to be holy, and to seek to struggle against that which is not holy and to embrace those attitudes that are. It is not so much what we do but why we do it. It is not just the choices that we make but the condition of our hearts in making those choices. If our heart is right and our desires are Godly, we will not go too far wrong in making the right choices.

Holiness is not so much the choices that we make but the condition of our hearts in making those choices.

But this is no mere option; it is not a choice we can make on the road to maturity. It is a requirement: it is a path we embrace in the light of the fear of God.

Philippians 2:12-15

> *"Therefore, my dear friends, as you have always obeyed – not only in my presence, but now much more in my absence – continue to work out your salvation with fear and trembling, for it is God who works in you to will and to act according to his good purpose.*
>
> *Do everything without complaining or arguing, so that you may become blameless and pure, children of God without fault in a crooked and depraved generation, in which you shine like stars in the universe."*

What picture do we have of the idea of the "Holy" Spirit?

The word "holy" is more than just a description of the Spirit; it is more than just saying that the Spirit Himself is set apart for God.

Wherever the Spirit is becomes holy. But holiness is a quality, and an internal attitude. It is clear that we do not become immediately holy when we embrace Christ; we may do so in the sense that we are redeemed before God but for us to make the journey towards internal holiness is an effort and sacrifice (Romans 7).

Holiness is a requirement: it is a path to be embraced in the light of the fear of God.

The Holy Spirit demands holiness.

And this is what the Spirit demands. He is the "Holy" Spirit not just in the sense that he is holy, and not just in the sense that he makes "holy" but also in the sense that he demands holiness. He is altogether holy, separate in every way to God; he is God. Any work, relationship, baptism, partnership, gift, fruit or calling will both lead to *and demand* "holiness."

In the Old Testament the place where Moses stood was holy because the Spirit was there. Moses had to participate in the holiness by taking off his shoes. The holiness of the Spirit did not take his shoes off for him! The Spirit made the ground holy and demanded that Moses reciprocated. So it is in the New Testament. The Spirit is a spirit of internal attitudes, set apart to honour God. He both births the desire for such attitudes in us but demands that we embrace and seek the same. There is no room for the Spirit in a walk with God that does not embrace his values.

Holiness is *the* attitude of the Spirit. To live a Christian life that is Spirit empowered is to live a holy life. Anything else is a sham; the authority of the Spirit is often imitated but nothing fools God.

Holiness can be summed up as something that is set apart for God, either by him or for him, and is endued with God's ownership. God himself is described as holy.

It is not difficult for us to understand why the Holy Spirit is called holy. The challenge for us is to see that God intends us to be holy. We can only be holy by taking on the nature of God.

This is something that we will never achieve in this life but we can aspire to it and rest in his grace where we fall short. I see holiness as two issues:

* The desire to achieve holy living in daily life
* The achieving of a measure of holy living in daily life

Holiness can be summed up as something that is set apart for God, either by him or for him, and is endued with God's ownership. God himself is described as holy.

There is no doubt that we can achieve a measure of holiness and that such holiness gives power and authority to our lives as well as great joy. But God does not intend us to live in the guilt of our failure to be holy and, by his grace, he also blesses us if we have the desire to be holy.

This may be a little like giving up smoking, and loosing weight. Nearly every smoker or individual who has had "those comments" made to them by their doctor has a desire to stop smoking and loose weight. However, the desire alone is not enough (unfortunately). Some real effort must come from the desire if there is to be any success. Holiness is similar. God does not only require the desire but he demands the effort that needs to go with the desire.

There are three stages for those who wish to give up smoking: stage one is finding the desire to give up; stage two is marrying the desire with the effort, desire alone is not sufficient; stage three is the getting there! Holiness is similar, we have three stages: the desire to be holy; the doing something about it; and the achievement of a measure of holiness in our lives.

Without doubt, God blesses those who achieve a measure of holiness in their lives. Without doubt, he blesses those who are trying and without doubt, he blesses those who only desire. The degree of his blessing is between him and the individual.

We do not seek to be holy because we want a reward; we seek to be holy because a desire for holiness is put within us by God's Spirit.

But we do not seek to be holy because we want a reward; we seek to be holy because a desire for holiness is put within us by God's Spirit. Meditate on the vine and the branches again. We cannot live in the fullness of the Spirit without a desire and effort to be holy. We cannot be holy without the help of the Spirit.

But what is holiness? Some see it as a perception of morality. I see it as adopting the nature of God. It is not only what we do or do not do, it is an inner environment of godliness that leads to godly behaviour. The Holy Spirit tells us what holiness is: it is love, joy, peace, patience, kindness, goodness, faithfulness, gentleness and self-control (Galatians 5:22-23). Other passages in the scripture instruct us as to how we should aim to behave. Central to Christian behaviour is the idea of being set apart for God.

The Holy Sprit will lead us into holiness, being separate for God. He will lead us into the correct moral decisions. These will be as the scripture teaches because scripture is given by the Spirit (2Timothy 3:16).

If we want more of the Spirit we should seek holiness.

If we get more of the Spirit we will become more holy.

We cannot find holiness without the Spirit.

We will not find the Spirit working without a call to holiness.

He is the HOLY Spirit, this is both his nature and his effect.

Chapter 6

He Will Baptise You!

"He, yes he, will baptise you in the Holy Spirit!"
Mark 1:8

* The impact that this statement of John's would have had on his hearers
* What this statement would raise in the mind of the hearers
* Who is he to send the Spirit – that is only done by God?
* How can we receive the Spirit – we are not worthy?

The Bible is a book of many cultures and maybe this is no truer than when Biblical east meets Biblical west. The Old Testament, written predominantly in Hebrew, approaches the world from a very different perspective than does the New, written in Greek. There is a world of difference between the Greek rhetorical analytical view of Paul in Romans and the descriptive and poetic properties employed in the Old Testament in the Hebrew language, as in the Psalms. Greek developed into an analytical tool whereas Hebrew developed into a descriptive tool.

Not to push this point too far but it is similar to the old story of what happens if you ask a chemist and a poet to describe a picture. One would say how big it was and what it was made of whereas the other would describe what it meant. If we allow our two mythical experts, the poet and the chemist, to be fluent in two languages, Greek and Hebrew, then, probably, the chemist would choose to write his report in Greek and the poet in Hebrew. This is not to say that one could not write a poem in Greek or a technical report in Hebrew, as there are many of both. It is to make the point that the ancient Hebrew speakers saw the world in terms of pictures, similes and comparisons whereas the ancient Greeks produced our tradition of logic.

The New Testament is a meeting place of these two traditions. They meet in Paul, who, as a "Hebrew of Hebrews" also wrote with the trained Greek analytical logic. Today, the Greek approach almost completely immerses us. We see almost everything in terms of questions that must have answers rather than in pictures containing various shades of meaning.

John the Baptist was a Hebrew. He thought like a Hebrew and he spoke to Hebrews. So was Jesus, who taught in parables, not in questions with right or wrong answers. Maybe we, rather than asking the question "What does the phrase 'The Baptism in the Holy Spirit' mean?" should ask the question "What picture does it paint?"

John the Baptist was a Hebrew. He thought like a Hebrew and he spoke to Hebrews. So was Jesus, who taught in parables not in questions with right or wrong answers.

Consider the frame and the canvas and then the colours of this picture.

John the Baptist strode, timely and God sent, into the pages of history. He came to a hungry, expectant and confused people. The question *"When will the kingdom be restored?"* was uppermost in the minds of those who looked for the restoration of the Jewish nation (and was asked of Jesus right up to and including the time of his ascension). It seemed as if all Israel, and many Gentiles, had flocked to John. John was not an empty man in a desert; he was an event, a laser of hope, a fracture in time; a man who spoke for God. To the pious he was expected, if not a little overdue. They had been praying for, hoping for and waiting for a deliverer since the return from exile to Jerusalem. John fitted the bill.

Rather than ask the question "What does the phrase 'The Baptism in the Holy Spirit' mean?" perhaps we should ask the question "What picture does it paint?"

About four hundred turbulent terrible years earlier, the Jews had returned to Jerusalem from exile in Babylon. Their history had been recorded in the scriptures, which were available and translated into Greek.[56] They believed that they had learnt the one lesson that mattered. In the beginning, God had made a covenant with them. This covenant depended on their keeping his laws. They knew that for thousands of years their fathers had flirted with God's judgement, profaned his laws and turned from his ways. Finally, God had judged them, taken away their nation, and placed them in captivity in Babylon for seventy years. After that seventy years, some of them, a remnant, had been able to return to Jerusalem as a

[56] The Septuagint, which was the scriptures that Jesus quoted.

weak and externally governed people. Nevertheless, they also knew that God had promised to restore his people as a full and free nation. Their understanding was that this would occur if they returned to keeping his laws. For four hundred years, from the captivity until John, they had been endeavouring to do this. During that time, their land had become the crossroads of the super powers; great empires had come and gone. They had formed allegiances and cultural ties. They had had times of blessings, times of terrible persecutions, times of relative independence, times of unity and times of division but they had not become an independent secure sovereign nation. At the time of John, things were changing again. The Romans had come about ninety years earlier. There was an accommodation of power between the Romans and the Jewish ruling classes but no great love of Rome, who when she walked into the Jewish arena had profaned the Temple. To the pious Jew God would restore Israel again as long as they kept the Law.

And could this be the time? There was political change and a strong national identity. The nation, led by the example of the Pharisees, strove to keep the law. There were the promises of God, the Temple worship with its authority and political power and now, after four hundred years of silence, a prophet, a prophet unlike any other: one whose authority and presence would make it easy to accept that he was the voice in the wilderness foretold by no less than Isaiah. One, who when later described as the greatest of all prophets and the Elijah that was to come could carry such acknowledgement without a question being raised. Here, at last, was a prophet who told them what to do and what to expect. What to do: they were to repent, but not as they had been, now they were to repent with a true heart-felt change because, John proclaimed, the longed for kingdom of God was near.

Such a message was expected, embraced, and yearned for. The kingdom was coming! John was welcomed with his message of spiritual revolution and spiritual food. For a while, it would seem as if John was the prophet of Moses, the anointed one. In the midst of this excitement, this revolution, this revival of hope and hoped for power; from within this national cry of presumptive victory, John declared that he was not the one; he was the herald.

And this is what he said:

> *"I baptise you with water for repentance. But after me will come one who is more powerful than I, whose sandals I am not fit to carry. He will baptise you with the Holy Spirit and with fire,"* Matthew 3:11.

This statement is so important that each of the four evangelists open their gospels with it. It forms the canvas of our picture.

Jesus closes his teaching with it.

Acts 1:4-8

> *"On one occasion, while he was eating with them, he gave them this command: 'Do not leave Jerusalem, but wait for the gift my Father promised, which you have heard me speak about. For John baptised with water, but in a few days you will be baptised with the Holy Spirit.' So when they met together, they asked him, 'Lord, are you at this time going to restore the kingdom to Israel?' He said to them: 'It is not for you to know the times or dates the Father has set by his own authority. But you will receive power when the Holy Spirit comes on you; and you will be my witnesses in Jerusalem, and in all Judea and Samaria, and to the ends of the earth.'"*

These words, in John's mouth, at that time, are nuclear in their impact and meaning. At the time they were not understood, as was

John's teaching per se, but if we are to understand the meaning and message of the gospel we need to see these words in the context in which God placed them, both in history, and in the scripture.

John came as a herald to proclaim that Jesus will baptise us in the Holy Spirit. And we, not being Greek speakers miss out on the power and emphasis of his words.[57] To the Hebrew listeners the Holy Spirit could only be sent by God and sent only to the great prophets. That John should say someone was going to send the Spirit to *them* was revolutionary if not unthinkable. But John emphasises his words by stressing "he" to ensure his point is made.[58] We could paraphrase John's declaration as follows.

"He, yes he, will baptise *you* in the Holy Spirit!"

This must raise the following questions in the mind of the hearers, "Who is he to send the Spirit – this can only done by God?" and "How can we receive the Spirit –we are not worthy?"

That is the frame and the canvass of our picture. The frame is the political and social expectation of the day. The canvas is John and his teaching. This message is so important that it is the purpose for Jesus coming.

Let us not make the mistake of asking what it means – yet. This is a statement made by the greatest of all Old Covenant prophets to a Hebrew audience. Let us ask what picture it paints, what story it brings.

---

[57] As we have previously noted John spoke in Aramaic and the scriptures are given to us in Greek. The gospel writers have deliberately reported John's words to us with these stresses.

[58] Matthew, Mark and Luke are almost identical. They report John as inserting the pronoun *autos* ("he") with the verb *baptisei* ("he will baptise"). The gospel of John also uses emphatic language.

"He, yes he, will baptise *you* in the Holy Spirit!"

This must raise the following questions in the mind of the hearers, "Who is he to send the Spirit – that is only done by God?" and "How can we receive the Spirit – we are not worthy?"

Let us look at the colours that are used.

Matthew 3:11	He will baptise you with the Holy Spirit and with fire.
Mark 1:8	He will baptise you with the Holy Spirit"
Luke 3:16	He will baptise you with the Holy Spirit and with fire.
John 1:33	I would not have known him, except that the one who sent me to baptise with water told me, "The man on whom you see the Spirit come down and remain is he who will baptise with the Holy Spirit."[59]

Two references say "with fire." We see the fire in the picture of the Shekinah and on the Day of Pentecost.[60] The primary colours of the picture are therefore:

---

[59] All quotes form NIV

[60] Shekinah, see Chapter 3

He	-	that is Jesus
Will	-	denoting his intention and resolve
Baptise	-	denoting what the picture is about
You *en* (in)	-	denoting what is happening to you
the Spirit	-	denoting who is involved with you
Holy	-	denoting what the effect is

We have covered these colours in the preceding chapters. All we need to do now is to take time to consider what we see and to appreciate the impression that we get of the intention of the one who instructed John.

He

The picture is one in which Jesus is the prime instigator; it is Jesus who is taking the initiative. In all the pictures we are given of a baptism there is one who is baptising and those who are baptised. The decision to baptise, the time and place all belong to Jesus. He is the dominant person in this picture.

Will

Not might, or could, but will. This is both a promise and a commitment. All pictures of baptism are conditional on certain criteria having been met. Once they are met, he will baptise. The criteria are not difficult to see. John came preaching repentance, which was the condition of his baptism. Jesus preached repentance. If we are to take this picture in its whole context, it must contain the condition of repentance. The promise is made to those who are still in their sins. If it is to come to its fulfilment then there must be repentance.

Baptise

We have seen baptism as a concept that contains a number of ideas. These include the idea of an initiation into a new spiritual life after a period of journeying or repentance. In the case of Israel in the desert it was a physical journey that allowed the old ways to die out and a new generation to emerge. This new generation would embrace the crossing of the Jordan into the new land. John's baptism was a token in recognition of a spiritual journey. This journey started with conviction that led to repentance that was sealed in washing. We understand Jesus redemptive ministry as a baptism of suffering, a process in which there is a new and different endpoint, in this case, for all humanity. In the days after his resurrection water baptism was the initiation into the new life and demands of the body of believers. The ideas of journeying, initiation, change and cost are core to this picture.

En

As the branch and the vine are one, yet separate, so we who are baptised in this way will be one with the Spirit, and thus with God, yet still individuals. We bear the fruit that is nourished and given by the Spirit. It is a picture of grafting; a vine has wild branches grafted into it, becoming one with it, and bearing its fruit.

The Spirit

We are not given a spirit to adopt as our own; we are grafted into the Holy Spirit.[61] The Father, who instructed John, gave us his Son for our redemption and then through the Son baptises us *en* his

---

[61] Jesus is the vine and we are the branches. The picture that I find useful is that of the Holy Spirit as the sap in the vine. As we are grafted into the vine, that is Jesus, we are also grafted into the sap. Chapter 2 reminds us that God is one.

Spirit. That he should do this and what exactly it means is beyond our human comprehension. We can only look, wonder and receive.

Holy

The final stage of the journey will be holiness as his Spirit is holy. The picture reveals only the past shadows of sin and rebellion left behind through repentance, those spectres being lost forever, invisible against the ineffable radiance of his holiness.

Chapter 7

The Teaching of Jesus in John

"But the Counsellor, the Holy Spirit, whom the Father will send in my name, he will teach you all things, and bring to your remembrance all that I have said to you."
John 14:26 RSV

* **John 14-15**
  The Father will send the Spirit in my name. He will testify of me
* **John 16**
  The three-fold ministry of the Spirit: to convict the world of guilt in regard to sin, righteousness and judgement
* **John 3**
  You must be born again; this is a work of the Spirit
* **John 7**
  The Spirit will be received from Jesus
* **John 20**
  The Spirit is received from Jesus

Jesus' baptism by John was significant both for him and for us. The Father spoke to him, the Spirit descended upon him, and it was the time that he heard John saying to the crowds that he, Jesus, would baptise them in the Holy Spirit. It is unthinkable that this was news to Jesus. John clearly says that the one who told him to baptise in water also told him to proclaim that Jesus would baptise in the Spirit: John learnt this from God. Jesus says that he and the Father are one so we can be certain that Jesus knew of his calling to baptise in the Spirit from within his relationship with the Father, not through John.

But not so the others who heard John. Many of Jesus' disciples were former disciples of John and they would remember this promise and look to Jesus to teach about it, which he did.

Acts 1:4-5

"On one occasion, while he was eating with them, he gave them this command: 'Do not leave Jerusalem, but wait for the gift my Father promised, which ***you have heard me speak about****. For John baptised with water, but in a few days you will be baptised with the Holy Spirit.'"*

Where is this teaching, and is it available to us?

It is interwoven throughout the Gospels and it becomes clear as soon as we start to see that the "Baptism in the Spirit" is not so much an event, or even a picture, but something that we can describe as a story, or an initiation, a passage, a journey, a baptism, all of which describes the context of a relationship.

The Gospel of John assigns teaching on the Spirit into five main sections:

* John and the statements concerning the Baptism in the Spirit; which we have already looked at
* The teaching to Nicodemus in John 3
* The statement in John 7
* The discourse around the identification of the Spirit as the *paraklet* in John 14-16
* And finally the "Johanine Pentecost" in John 20

It is unnecessary and unnatural to divorce these teachings from others concerning the Spirit. When all these teachings are taken together, what emerges is a consistent whole.

Jesus' teaching concerning the Holy Spirit is interwoven throughout the Gospels and it becomes clear as soon as we start to see it within the context of a relationship.

John 14-15

From the teaching in John 14-15 we can paraphrase the following:

> *"And I will ask the Father, and he will give you another Counsellor to be with you forever – the Spirit of truth. The world cannot accept him, because*

it neither sees him nor knows him. But you know him, for he dwells in you (en) and shall be close to you (par) and amongst you (meta). The Father will send him in my name, he will teach you all things and will remind you of everything I have said to you. He will testify about me."

Firstly we can see that it is Jesus who asks the Father to send the Spirit and the Spirit is sent in Jesus' name; so Jesus is the initiator, the baptiser. Next we can see that the Spirit is only given to the believers so becoming a believer is part of this story. The Spirit is to dwell both alongside and amongst the believers in this world (*par* and *meta*) and he is to be *en* them.[62] When the Spirit is *en* them, he will both teach them all things as well as directing them to the teachings of Jesus.

It is unnecessary and unnatural to divorce teachings concerning the Spirit. When all teachings are taken together what emerges is a consistent whole.

John 16:7-14

"But I tell you the truth: It is for your good that I am going away. Unless I go away, the Counsellor will not come to you; but if I go, I will send him to you. When he comes, he will convict the world of guilt in regard to sin and righteousness and judgement: in

[62] John 14:16-17 , *meta* carries the idea of among, *para* carries the idea of physically close to, or near. Chapter 4 has discussed *en*.

regard to sin, because men do not believe in me; in regard to righteousness, because I am going to the Father, where you can see me no longer; and in regard to judgement, because the prince of this world now stands condemned. I have much more to say to you, more than you can now bear. But when he, the Spirit of truth, comes, he will guide you into all truth. He will not speak on his own; he will speak only what he hears, and he will tell you what is yet to come. He will bring glory to me by taking from what is mine and making it known to you."

Here we have a three-fold ministry of the Spirit, to convict the world of guilt in regard to sin, righteousness and judgement.

Sin

The Spirit will raise the guilt of sin in the heart of those who do not believe in Jesus; the Spirit, in this context, convicts the world of sin. This would be a future believer's first experience of the Spirit. There is a time and process in the lives of believers when they became aware of sin. The sinner became a pilgrim who sought to find an answer to this plight. It is found at the cross, the forgiveness of sins, bought and given by the life, death and resurrection of Christ. To lead an individual into this process is the work of the Spirit, the first work that the Spirit does in the believer.

Righteousness

Why is there a need to convict of righteousness? Because Jesus is leaving the world and going to the Father. The pilgrim, now forgiven and free from the guilt of sin, must live in this world without the presence of Jesus. It is the Spirit who guides him in his walk with God, showing and convicting him of the need not just to avoid sin, but to embrace God's values and to live in joyful harmony with them. This then becomes the walk of the Christian and the Spirit, the Spirit *en* the Christian.

> **There is a three-fold ministry of the Spirit: to convict the world of guilt in regard to sin, righteousness and judgement.**

Judgement

The Spirit will bring a message of judgement, because evil is already judged.[63] This is not a message of condemnation to those who, through this work of the Spirit, are God's; to them it is a message of comfort and victory as evil is already condemned. To those who do not embrace Christ but who choose to reject him, it is a message of inevitable judgement. To paraphrase Paul, to one, it is the sweet smell of salvation, to the other the stench of death.[64]

---

[63] Romans 1:18
The wrath of God *is being* revealed from heaven against all the godlessness and wickedness of men who suppress the truth by their wickedness. (NIV)

[64] 2 Corinthians 2:16

This passage also brings to the fore one of the characteristics of the Spirit. Jesus said that the Spirit would bring glory to him. There is no tension in the Godhead; the Spirit will always glorify the Son. It is his delight and pleasure to do so.

John 3:3

In reply Jesus declared, *"I tell you the truth, no one can see the kingdom of God unless he is born again."*

It is clear from this passage that to be born again is a work of the Spirit and it is self-evident that Jesus is talking about salvation. If we see the Baptism in the Spirit as a journey that unfolds before us then the imagery of being born of the Spirit is another picture for entering *en* the Spirit. In the pictures that we have of Baptism there are certain key moments, entering the water, going through the water, and coming up from the water. In the "Baptism of Moses" there is the leaving of Egypt, the journeying in the desert and the entering of the Promised Land after going through Jordan. In Christ's ministry there is Gethsemane, the Crucifixion and the Resurrection. It is the role of the Spirit to convict the sinner of sin and to lead him to Christ. It is the continuation of this process for the Spirit to lead the sinner through to repentance and to the acceptance of Christ as his Saviour.

John 3:14-18

> *"Just as Moses lifted up the snake in the desert, so the Son of Man must be lifted up, that everyone who believes in him may have eternal life.*
>
> *For God so loved the world that he gave his one and only Son, that whoever believes in him shall not perish but have eternal life. For God did not send his*

Son into the world to condemn the world, but to save the world through him. Whoever believes in him is not condemned, but whoever does not believe stands condemned already because he has not believed in the name of God's one and only Son."

If we see the Baptism in the Spirit as a journey that unfolds before us then the imagery of being born of the Spirit is another picture for entering *en* the Spirit.

It is only through the work of the Spirit that a person, who is an enemy of God, one who is lost in sin and living in rebellion to God, can come to such a saving belief. Such an individual's first contact with the Spirit will be in recognising guilt and sin. However, the Spirit does not leave the pilgrim there; the Spirit leads him on to Christ giving the sinner opportunity to find forgiveness and eternal life. The journey does not even stop there as the Spirit leads on to greater things!

John 7:37-40

"*On the last and greatest day of the Feast, Jesus stood and said in a loud voice, 'If anyone is thirsty, let him come to me and drink. Whoever believes in me, as the Scripture has said, streams of living water will flow from within him.'*

By this he meant the Spirit, whom those who believed in him were later to receive. Up to that time the Spirit had not been given, since Jesus had not yet been glorified."

When the work of the Spirit is complete those who have received this Baptism will flow with blessings. The Greek word translated as "receive" is *lambano*, which we will discover more about later on.[65] For now, we can see that the work of the Spirit in this baptism is to take an individual who is in rebellion to God and then to convict such an individual of sin and lead him through to salvation. But the end point of this journey is not to merely escape God's wrath and to receive an eternal pardon. It is to become a partner *en* the Spirit, becoming, as if it were, a stream of living water, flowing with blessing and being as one with the Spirit in his work.

What begins to emerge from the scripture is that the Baptism in the Spirit is a Baptism in which the baptised is found as a rebel in sin and turned into a true and effective servant of God. There are key stages in this journey: coming under the conviction of sin and recognising sin for what it is, enmity with God; being taken to the cross and responding with repentance and receiving forgiveness; and finally; being led forward into a life of righteousness and effective service, empowered by the same Spirit and endued with spiritual gifts. It is not sufficient to stay at the cross; to receive pardon is only part of the blessing.

When the work of the Spirit is complete those who have received this Baptism will flow with blessings.

John 20:21-22

> *"Again Jesus said, 'Peace be with you! As the Father has sent me, I am sending you.' And with that*

[65] See chapter 8.

> *he breathed on them and said, 'Receive (labete – lambano) the Holy Spirit.'"*

After his resurrection Jesus appeared to the disciples on a number of occasions. On this occasion, he breathed on them saying that they should receive the Spirit. This poses a number of problems if we take the view that the Baptism in the Spirit is an event rather than a process as this would put this account in John at variance with the account in Acts. Furthermore, as not all the disciples were there (Thomas, one of the twelve, was absent) it would raise the question of a private or another outpouring. Other explanations, such as describing this as the point at which some received salvation, cause more problems than are solved. If we see the Baptism in the Spirit as the work of the Spirit from conviction to servant-hood there is no problem as this is part of the continuing process. This again demonstrates the central role of Jesus in the endowing of the Spirit. We are shown a picture that confirms this as an ongoing process, and, by implication, that we may continue to need the breath of the Son of God upon us.

Chapter 8

The Day of Pentecost

"But you will receive power when the Holy Spirit comes on you; and you will be my witnesses in Jerusalem, and in all Judea and Samaria, and to the ends of the earth."
Acts 1:8 (NIV)

* The events of the day of Pentecost in the light of Luke's language and experience
* The Greek word *lambano*
* Luke's observation of the Spirit coming upon individuals
* Luke's use of the phrase "Baptised in the Spirit"

Right at the end of Jesus' ministry on earth, he returns to the purpose of his coming as given by John the Baptist. Jesus directed the disciples' thoughts to John's declaration.

> *"On one occasion, while he was eating with them, he gave them this command: 'Do not leave Jerusalem, but wait for the gift my Father promised, which you have heard me speak about. For John baptised with water, but in a few days you will be baptised with the Holy Spirit,'"* Acts 1:4-5.

They, still not understanding the exact nature of Jesus ministry, asked about the restoring of the physical kingdom of Israel. He replied:

> *"It is not for you to know the times or dates the Father has set by his own authority.*[66] *But you will receive power when the Holy Spirit comes on you; and you will be my witnesses in Jerusalem, and in all Judea and Samaria, and to the ends of the earth. After he said this, he was taken up before their very eyes, and a cloud hid him from their sight,"* Acts 1:7-9.

Before we look at this, let us remind ourselves that these are the last words of Jesus on earth, his last command to us. This fact alone must give his instructions some importance.

We have been trying to understand what John the Baptist meant by the statement "He will baptise you in the Holy Spirit." The picture continues to develop as we consider its revelations in the hands of Luke. Luke was probably a Gentile physician trained in such arts by the Greeks. He wrote easily and fluently in Greek. He was probably based in Troy and was one of Paul's travelling companions. He appears to have been a life long friend of Paul's and we must

---

[66] This is not to deny that he would restore the kingdom, but a statement that humanity will live within God's sovereignty.

assume that he and Paul spent many days, if not months in prayer and conversation about the things of God.[67] It is inconceivable that he and Paul had any significant difference in their views considering the time that they spent together and Paul's clarity of expression. It is safe to assume that they had the same view of the Baptism in the Holy Spirit.

Luke wrote the Gospel of Luke and Acts. In order to construct a coherent account of Luke's research we may conclude that he spent some time in Jerusalem. Whether this was before, during or after his travels with Paul is difficult to say but we do have Luke's own account of this research.

> *"Many have undertaken to draw up an account of the things that have been fulfilled among us, just as they were handed down to us by those who from the first were eyewitnesses and servants of the word. Therefore, since I myself have carefully investigated everything from the beginning, it seemed good also to me to write an orderly account for you, most excellent Theophilus, so that you may know the certainty of the things you have been taught,"* Luke 1:1-4.

We can make a few firm conclusions from this:

1. "Things" had been done in Luke's presence
2. Luke was not one of the original disciples
3. The things that were done were consistent with the teaching that had been handed down
4. Luke, personally, had made a careful investigation and had prepared an orderly account

[67] Consider the implications of 2 Timothy 4:11.

We can assume that Luke's definition of "careful" owes something to his Greek training. He clearly links Acts with his Gospel and we are safe in making these same assumptions for Acts.

> *"In my former book, Theophilus, I wrote about all that Jesus began to do and to teach until the day he was taken up to heaven, after giving instructions through the Holy Spirit to the apostles he had chosen,"* Acts 1:1-2.

This is a careful account and we can be precise about Luke's language and concepts. We would, of course, be making a big mistake if we were to try to read concepts that we ourselves would wish to project into every nuance of language that Luke uses. Luke is not writing a systematic theology. He is presenting an accurate report of what he saw and heard. In his mind, these events are orderly and coherent. He shows us no incredulity at what happened so we can assume that things happened in a way that had become usual to Luke. In other words, by the time Luke came to write Acts he was familiar with these events and he was seeing things as occurring to a pattern. We are still seeing this as a picture but we may assume that Luke is using a finer brush. So, before we look at the brush strokes, let us look at the brushes. What we are going to do is to see if there are any clues as to how Luke saw the colours of the picture, we are going to try to see things as he did.

In Acts, Luke appears to address events relating to the Spirit in three ways:

He uses the wider concept of "came upon" or "filled."

He uses *"lambano"* (receive).

He uses the phrase "Baptism in the Spirit."

By the time Luke came to write Acts he was familiar with these events and he was seeing things as occurring to a pattern.

"Came upon"

Luke describes situations in which the Spirit comes upon an individual.[68] He uses a number of different words to describe this, all with meanings that imply "come upon", "filling" or "falling upon", or "poured out upon."[69] Each time Luke paints this picture there is either the expectation or the fact that there is an outward manifestation of the Spirit's working. In each of these examples, those observing are able to tell that the Spirit has fallen on the individual because the individual shows outward evidence of that having happened. We can assume then, that Luke is familiar with an experience of the Spirit in which the Spirit comes upon an individual and that individual outwardly manifests the Spirit's presence. He does not seem to attempt to explain what is happening, or even why, he just paints a picture of it happening.

---

[68] John, Mary, Elizabeth, Zechariah and Simeon. See the discussion later in this chapter.

[69] In his gospel we have similar expressions as with John (1:15), Mary (1:35), Elizabeth (1:41), Zechariah (1:67) and Simeon (2:25). The words he uses are similar to those used in Acts. These pre-resurrection involvements with the Spirit cannot be seen as part of our involvement with the Spirit as Jesus clearly said that after he had returned to the Father the Spirit would be sent in a different way, which the disciples were still waiting for in the first chapter of Acts.

These words do give us an understanding of what it meant to be visited by the Spirit in the pre-resurrection era. There is a continuity of experience; what happened before the resurrection happens afterwards but in a more powerful way.

Those observing are able to tell that the Spirit has fallen on an individual because the individual shows outward evidence of that having happened.

"Lambano"

The next consistency from Luke is his use of the word *lambano*.[70] This is almost universally translated as "receive" but we will be well rewarded if we consider this in a little more detail. A very cursory examination of modern popular Greek dictionaries will show that this word can also be translated "to take" or even "to seize", and maybe even should be translated as "to take" or "to seize".[71] Thayer's 1993 has the following entry:

---

[70] Further occasions where *lambano* is used are discussed in following chapters.

[71] Greek is no different from any other language in that it is acceptable for a word to be occasionally used outside of its normal contextual range. Some may suggest that *lambano* can be translated as "receive" under this license. In order to use a word outside of its usual contextual range would need good reasons and there are no such reasons in this case. *Lambano* is not an uncommon word in the New Testament and it is used particularly frequently in passages relating to the Spirit. There is never a reason, in any of these occasions, to translate it as "receive" rather than "to take hold of" or seize. There are many examples in the gospels where *lambano* is translated as "receive". In many of these the idea of "seizing" is coherent with the text. In some the idea of "receiving" would seem to be preferred (Matt 7:8 for example). It would be wrong to suggest that *lambano* can only be translated as "seizing" , words are broad brushes, but "seizing" should be the preferred translation unless there is compelling textural support otherwise. It may be that the reason that so many Bible translators have used "receive" is that they have followed the tradition of previous translations. Whether this is evidence or not of the very earliest translators preferring nuances of meaning that fitted with the expectation of the ruling authorities at the time (i.e., that the individual was dependent upon the power of those authorities and could only "receive" when offered and did not have the spiritual right to "take") is not part of our discussion here.

- of that which when taken is not let go, to seize, to lay hold of, to apprehend

- to take by craft (our catch, used of hunters, fisherman, etc.), to circumvent one by fraud

- to take to oneself, to lay hold upon, to take possession of, that is, to appropriate to oneself

- to catch at, to reach after, to strive to obtain

- to take a thing due, to collect, to gather (tribute)

- to take

- to admit, to receive

- to receive what is offered

not to refuse or reject

- to receive a person, to give him access to oneself, to regard anyone's power, rank, external circumstances, and on that account to do some injustice or neglect something

- to take, to choose, to select

- to take beginning, to prove anything, to make a trial of, to experience

- to receive (what is given), to gain, to get, to obtain, to get back.

This meaning seems to require a lot more of an active role on behalf of the receiver than simply receiving! This is also the word that John uses when he gives us the picture of Jesus breathing on the disciples; was Jesus saying "take the Spirit" implying an act of will for the disciples rather than just "receive" whilst the Spirit was given as some sort of supernatural injection? "Taking" implies both an empowerment of the individual and a responsibility, in other words, there is the power to take and there must be a decision with an effort to take. "Receiving", implies that the power is only with the giver; "taking" implies a mutual act. ("Stealing", of course would imply a one way act but we do not have to steal, the gift is freely offered – if we take.)

When I was visiting an African country, I was invited to a party to celebrate the first birthday of a little girl. Her name, aptly, was Joy. It was an affair mainly for friends and family as Joy was, as yet, too young to invite her own peers and playmates. Gifts were brought and presented to the proud parents rather than to Joy, who was uncomprehending about much of the fuss. Each friend or relative would bring a well-presented parcel and show it to Joy but give it to the parents who, on Joy's behalf, would gladly receive it. The presents were Joy's and she had received them. Then a young bachelor arrived, a close friend of the father. He was evidently well known to Joy who recognised him and showed no unease at being passed to him to hold (unlike myself who she had immediately recognised as a stranger). After this greeting, the friend passed Joy back to her father. Then, with Joy's full attention on him, the friend slowly produced a long, floppy, big smiley-faced cuddly dolly and held her out in front of Joy, just out of her reach. Well, the effect was immediate. Joy's face lit up and she squealed that delightful sound that only a pleased one-year-old can make. She reached forward to try to take the dolly, her little legs kicking in excitement and her eyes fixed on the smiley face. The father and friend were delighted and as the father slowly brought Joy towards the doll and as the friend slowly brought the doll towards Joy, with her reach fully extended, she seized the doll with both hands and held it close to her body. The two, the doll and Joy, became inseparable for most of the evening. A few days later and now attributed with enough credibility for her to sit on my lap and play with me, I visited Joy at home. As we sat on the long settee, I noticed the doll at the end, just within my arms reach, so I stretched across, retrieved it and offered it to Joy. She took it from me and held it with a confidence and assurance that simply said, "That's mine!"

Joy had, through her parents, received every gift given to her but she had taken hold of the doll in the full sense of *lambano.* The gift had been given and placed before her. It was not given with any sense of condition or requirement, the sole purpose of it having been bought and brought was to give it to Joy and I doubt the friend had any other use for it. But she had reached out for it, she had taken it to herself, there was a sense of joy and delight in what was offered and in the way in which it was received.

Is there any other way in which Christians should receive the Spirit when He comes to us? In Luke's experience, the pouring out of the Spirit was met with some tangible change that was discernible to all around. I cannot see Paul's view being any different. In Paul's experience, it was the laying hold (*lambano*) of the Spirit that was the certain life-changing event *by which they could prove* the validity of what he had taught them.[72] It is clear that for Paul this experience was normal. I am not seeking to prove an exegetical point here, just to show the consistency of the emerging picture. In picture terms, there is an exaltation in the New Testament by which Christians are told to seize, take, lay hold of the Spirit and in which the Spirit is freely offered. It will not help us here to try and explain *what* is happening in terms of the spiritual processes going on between God and the believer.[73] What is important is to understand *that* it is happening.

---

[72] See chapter 14.

[73] This is explored in Part 2 – *The Traveller*.

Some may find such a picture to be too bold and assertive. However, the picture is not of the human individual taking from God at the will and instigation of the individual. And neither is it a picture of God overpowering and controlling the recipient.[74] It is a picture of the Holy Spirit being offered, according to God's sovereign will and plan, and the offer being taken up eagerly by the recipient. Such a transaction takes place in the context of a relationship. Here is the mystery, the sovereign will of God, by which the gift of the Spirit is offered, taken up by the exercise of the free will of his created being. God, in his sovereign grace offers, we, in humility have the responsibility to accept.

> **"*Lambano,*" which is translated "receive", can also be translated "to take hold of".**

The Baptism in the Spirit

Luke only uses this term a few times. It is as important to see when he does not use it as it is to see when he uses it.

> *"For John baptised with water, but in a few days you will be baptised with the Holy Spirit,"* Acts 1:5.

This clearly refers to the Day of Pentecost when, for the disciples, they will have been baptised in the Spirit. This verse does not necessarily mean that the whole process takes place on that day, only that on that day it will be complete. We can compare this with a degree ceremony. On the day of graduation, the candidate receives the degree. One could say to them, "You will receive your

---

[74] This can occur when the individual is under judgement.

degree on the day of graduation." Nevertheless, the degree would have taken some years to complete.

> *"But you will receive power when the Holy Spirit comes on you; and you will be my witnesses in Jerusalem, and in all Judea and Samaria, and to the ends of the earth,"* Acts 1:8.

This refers to the day of Pentecost as well but it directly tells us what happens on that day. There is no inference that the process of this baptism takes place all on that one day, rather there is a description of what will happen to them on that day. They will take hold of power when the Spirit comes upon them. This power will enable them to be effective witnesses.[75]

> *"Then I remembered what the Lord had said: 'John baptised with water, but you will be baptised with the Holy Spirit,'"* Acts 11:16.

This is the end of the account where Peter visits the house of Cornelius, a Gentile. Whilst Peter was speaking the Spirit was poured out upon them and they took up the opportunity of the Spirit. The Spirit came upon them while Peter was speaking about the forgiveness of sin through believing in Jesus. It seems self evident that these people, to use John's words, had become born again, repenting of their sins while Peter spoke and that the Holy Spirit had been poured out upon them. They had taken hold of the

[75] In verse 5, the verb for "you will be baptised" is passive, in other words they are baptised by another. In verse 8, the word translated as "you will receive" is *lambano* in a middle voice, in other words, this implies some action from those receiving (to act upon themselves).

Spirit and were manifesting signs of spiritual power and awakening. That this had happened was a point of some incredulity to the other apostles, so much so that Peter had had to give them an explanation. It seems that the difficulty for the other apostles was that the gentiles had received salvation and thus were equal to them in the eyes of God (Acts 11:3). Luke reports that Peter describes the whole process, of seeking, hearing, believing, repenting, outpouring, receiving and using the spiritual power, as the Baptism in the Holy Spirit.

> *"Then I remembered what the Lord had said: 'John baptised with water, but you will be baptised with the Holy Spirit.' So if God gave them the same gift as he gave us, who believed in the Lord Jesus Christ, who was I to think that I could oppose God?" When they heard this, they had no further objections and praised God, saying, 'So then, God has granted even the Gentiles repentance unto life,'"* Acts 11:16-18.

Luke reports that Peter describes the whole process, of seeking, hearing, believing, repenting, outpouring, receiving and using spiritual power, as the Baptism in the Holy Spirit.

Now we can see the brush strokes that Luke is using. In the light of this let us move on to see what appears to have happened on the Day of Pentecost and then what else happened in the rest of Acts. We are not looking for explanations as to what was happening in terms of spiritual dynamics, only a picture of what occurred and Luke's view of that picture.

We must start our journey with Luke in his gospel. Here he consistently describes the Spirit as coming upon an individual: John, Mary, Elizabeth, Zechariah and Simeon. The Spirit descended upon Jesus in the form of a dove and then led him into the wilderness. Jesus continues his ministry in the power of the Spirit promising the Spirit to those that seek him.

> *"If you then, though you are evil, know how to give good gifts to your children, how much more will your Father in heaven give the Holy Spirit to those who ask him!"* Luke 11:13.

The Spirit can be sinned against (Luke 12:10). It is the Spirit's role to teach and bring things to memory and recognition (Luke 12:12). Luke sees the Spirit very much like John in the role of a *paraklet*e, an advocate, he is someone with whom one interacts. He describes the Spirit as being in a relationship with those who were seeking him. It was the Spirit who revealed to Simeon that he would see the Christ and who the Christ was. It could only have been the Spirit who revealed to Peter that Jesus was the Christ. In Luke's account, the statement that Jesus would baptise *en* the Spirit would have been revolutionary. Luke shows that they knew of an experience in which the Spirit interacted with prophets, taught them, convicted them, and came upon them with effect, but the idea that the ordinary Jew could be *en* the Spirit would have been for them, a mind blowing concept. In Acts 1 Luke shows that the disciples had been in a relationship with the Spirit, there was nothing unusual about that. They were to wait for the Spirit to come upon them; there was nothing too unusual about that, it had happened to Mary (who was present, and whose presence would have reminded them of such) and others who were present on the Day of Pentecost and that is what happened, the Spirit came upon them, they were filled with the Spirit (Acts 2:4). Luke uses one of his "to be filled" words *pletho*. From the disciples perspective, as described by Luke, this was not an unusual or necessarily unexpected occurrence. At risk of sounding repetitious, let us say again, such things had happened before.[76] What was unusual was not that the Spirit came upon any of them, it was the context in which the Spirit came upon them.

Luke shows a number of things that made this pouring out different. Not the least was the presence of the tongues of fire that treated them all corporately as one body yet preserved their individuality. This is surely the return of the Shekinah, the Shekinah of the burning bush, of the Cherubim in the Tabernacle, that which was last given at the time of the Temple in the time of Solomon and taken away when the Temple was destroyed because of Israel's disobedience (Ezek.10: 18). This is the Shekinah that in its very essence, signifies the dwelling presence of God. The Holy Spirit had come to dwell, not along side but *en* the believers.

Then there was the effect of this out pouring. It would be hard to believe an encounter with the Spirit that was more life changing than that of Mary's at the conception or of the effect on Simeon or on Elizabeth. But this out pouring did not just change their destinies or what they knew; it changed them. Peter, an unlearned man, stood up and caused those around him not just to listen but to be astounded (Acts 4:13). They moved in an anointing of the Spirit that could only be termed as beyond their own natures, super-natured, gifted by the Spirit.

---

[76] Mary, Elizabeth, Zechariah, Simeon and John.

As Luke describes the disciples, from their perspective it would not have been an unusual event for the Spirit to come upon them on the day of Pentecost; such things had happened before, not the least to Mary. What was unusual was the context and the effect that this outpouring had had.

There was a prophetic direction to this outpouring. As Jesus had taught in John's gospel, they, *en* the Spirit, were to convict others of sin, righteousness and judgement. They were called to bring thousands to a saving knowledge of Christ. This demonstrated their power in the Gospel, a power they always attributed to Jesus.[77]

We cannot ignore the miraculous tongues. These, clearly, were miraculously spoken languages, unknown to the speakers but understood by others. This sign, often called xenolalia, appears to be clearly different from the speaking in other languages that are not understood by observers, which is often called glossolalia. Xenolalia is unique to the Day of Pentecost in the New Testament. It may be considered as prophetic; indicating that the gift poured out was for all people of all races, signifying the disciples' authority and responsibility to go to all nations.

This was the end of their initiation, the end of their pilgrimage from rebellious sinners to soldiers for God, called, convicted, purified, equipped and active: now they were *en* the Spirit, baptised and active for God.

[77] Acts 3:12-13,16 for example.

Chapter 9

The Events in Acts

"You will be my witnesses in Jerusalem, and in all Judea and Samaria, and to the ends of the earth."
Acts 1:8

* The events in Samaria in Acts 8
* The events in Caesarea in Acts 10
* The events in Ephesus in Acts 19

At his ascension, Jesus gave the disciples directions as to what they should do:

"But you will receive power when the Holy Spirit comes on you; and you will be my witnesses in Jerusalem, and in all Judea and Samaria, and to the ends of the earth," Acts 1:8.

Part of Luke's story is to show how this was worked out. For the Jews there were three different types of race, Jews, Samaritans and

Gentiles. The Jews were the first to receive the gift of the Holy Spirit that the Father had promised. The next would be the Samaritans and Luke records this event in Acts 8. He records the inclusion of the Gentiles in Acts 10 and that this should continue to the ends of the earth in Acts 19. It would be a mistake to consider that these were the only such episodes; absence of evidence is not evidence of absence. The presence of the gifts of the Spirit amongst the Corinthians and Romans and verses like Acts 9:17-18, Galatians 3:2 may also infer other such events.

Samaria

Following the persecution that broke out after Stephen's death, Philip, in Acts 8, went to Samaria, no doubt encouraged to do so by Jesus' frequent journeying and ministry there.[78] Following his preaching a revival broke out. If we are following Luke's expectations then this revival would consist of the evidence of the work of the Spirit. Luke would expect there to be a period of conviction, a time of believing and of repenting, and as in Acts 2 a submission to water baptism and a pouring out of the Spirit to equip the new Christians for their new life, values and calling. This is exactly what we see:

> *"But when they believed Philip as he preached the good news of the kingdom of God and the name of Jesus Christ, they were baptised, both men and women,"* Acts 8:12.

[78] John 4:1-42 for example.

It is absolutely inconceivable to consider that Philip was baptising them unless they had believed and repented. We have a full record of Peter's teaching on this in the early chapters of Acts and his statements on the Day of Pentecost. To consider that Philip had gone independent and ignored Peter's teaching is not tenable. We can be fairly certain that Luke was not an eyewitness to this revival but that his account had been carefully collected. It is of note then that Luke records that the Spirit had not been poured out upon them. To Luke this was significant, probably because he wishes us to observe that the problem was solved when the other apostles arrived.

They placed their hands upon the new converts and prayed. Why did they do this? It would appear that they also expected there to be a spiritual outpouring and had learnt what to do when it did not occur immediately. The further implication is that it did not always occur immediately. What followed was an outpouring in which it was clear to all around that the Spirit was active. The new converts received (*lambano*) the Spirit.[79]

For the moment let us just make the observation that we have a consistent stream of events. We may note the relationship between receiving the Spirit and external evidence (tongues and prophecy) and we may compare this with the Spirit coming upon Zechariah in Luke, Mary and Elizabeth, Simeon. In each case the interaction with the Spirit is confirmed by clear cut external evidence. Simeon's reaction shows that he had observed something that accompanied this outpouring of the Spirit, although Luke does not say what it was.

[79] In Acts 8:15 and 17 *lambano* is used. In Acts 8:18 the Greek word used translates easily as "given". The implication is that through the ministry of the apostles the Spirit was made available, or given, but the new Christians still needed to receive or take hold of the Spirit to complete the work.

We should also carefully note that the term "baptism" in this story is confined to the water initiation rite. The text does not identify the outpouring of the Spirit on these Samaritans as the Baptism in the Spirit. Verse 15 says that they had not yet taken hold (*lambano*) of the Spirit and verse 16 that the Spirit had not fallen upon them. In verse 17 the word used is *lambano*. The sense of the other verses is that Simon asked that the believers would take hold of the Spirit (*lambano*) when he laid his hands upon them. Nowhere in the text is this process called or equated to the Baptism in the Spirit. This was a taking hold of the Spirit, which, as we are seeing, is only part of the Baptism in the Spirit.

Caesarea

Acts 10 is similar and we have already largely discussed it.[80] What is important is to realise that this was the pouring out of the Spirit upon the Gentiles. Luke probably records this event as it shows the fulfilment of the command to take the Gospel *"to Jerusalem, and in all Judea and Samaria, and to the ends of the earth."* What Luke terms the Baptism of the Spirit contains elements of seeking, conviction, salvation, and an outpouring. As a process this had taken years with the disciples, days with the Samaritans and seems to have happened all within the course of one sermon with the Gentiles. There is no significance meant here in the comparative times that this took, only that the time taken and the process were different but that the constituent events were the same. It is worth repeating that Peter describes the whole processes of hearing, repenting, believing and of the Spirit coming upon them as the Baptism in the Spirit.[81]

---

[80] Chapter 8.

[81] Acts 11:14-17.

Ephesus

Luke details one more account that is of interest to us, that of the missed disciples in Ephesus. Paul had spent some years in Ephesus on his previous journey. It would appear that this time he had travelled in on a different route and found some disciples whom he, and probably, judging by their lack of understanding, the church in Ephesus, were unaware of. These were disciples but they had not been fully taught and their experience was incomplete. This may not have been an unusual occurrence at this time as much the same is hinted at with Apollos in the preceding chapter. In Acts there are places where Luke writes in the second person, "we" and where he writes about Paul in the third person "he." It is widely accepted that Luke was personally with Paul in the passages that are recorded as "we" and not in those that are recorded as "he." This part of Acts is a "he" part, so we may assume that Luke's account is gathered second hand from Paul.

> *"While Apollos was at Corinth, Paul took the road through the interior and arrived at Ephesus. There he found some disciples and asked them, "Did you receive the Holy Spirit when you believed?" They answered, "No, we have not even heard that there is a Holy Spirit." So Paul asked, "Then what baptism did you receive?" "John's baptism," they replied. Paul said, "John's baptism was a baptism of repentance. He told the people to believe in the one coming after him, that is, in Jesus." On hearing this, they were baptized into the name of the Lord Jesus. When Paul placed his hands on them, the Holy Spirit came on them, and they spoke in tongues and prophesied. There were about twelve men in all,"* Acts 19:1-7.

Why did Paul ask them the question *"Did you receive the Holy Spirit when you believed?"* and why did Luke record it?

We may conjecture that Paul, on meeting them, not only asked, "Are you saved?" but also asked, *"Did you receive the Holy Spirit when you believed?"* There seem to be two processes here. Firstly, Paul asked, *"Did you receive the Holy Spirit when you believed?"* and secondly, either Luke asked Paul if he had asked this question or Paul told him that he had. The important point is not only what the question asks but also what it implies.

Avoiding conjecture, what we know is:

* That these Ephesians were disciples. Luke tells us that this was Paul's understanding and I cannot see the wisdom in arguing with Paul over that, much the best course is to accept it on its face value [82]
* That they were not taught in apostolic doctrine knowing "only the Baptism of John"
* That they knew nothing of the Holy Spirit

Their state of knowledge at the beginning of their encounter with Paul is not important, what matters, is where they were at the end of it.

---

[82] What is not clear is what they believed or knew. Paul appears to introduce them to the one who was to follow John, namely Jesus. It may be that these were believers in the sense only that they were followers of John and had not even heard of Jesus. This would explain Luke's recording that Paul had to tell them that John told the people to believe in the one coming after him, that is, in Jesus. But this view would mean that we have an exceptional use of the word *mathetes* which is consistently used in the New Testament to mean "disciples" in the sense that we would use "Christian." Either way this is not important and I am inclined to think that if it were the Holy Spirit would have made the issue clearer for us.

What we can infer from this was that is was possible to be a disciple and not to have taken hold of the Spirit. This may not be as surprising as we think. It is clear that following Stephen's martyrdom there was a dispersion of the disciples, many of whom may not have received full apostolic instruction. What we can see for certain is that Paul's expectation for them, and by implication everyone else, was that they did take hold of the Spirit.[83] For Paul and Luke the key question was had they taken hold of the Spirit. This was the goal and the aim of their missionary endeavour.

---

[83] To develop this thought further, but, I must add, only through conjecture, we may look back at the end of the last chapter where Apollos seems to be in a not dissimilar state of teaching.

Acts 18:24-26
"A Jew named Apollos, a native of Alexandria, came to Ephesus. He was a learned man, with a thorough knowledge of the Scriptures. He had been instructed in the way of the Lord, and he spoke with great fervour and taught about Jesus accurately, though he knew only the baptism of John. And he began to speak boldly in the synagogue. When Priscilla and Aquila heard him, they invited him to their home and explained to him the way of God more adequately."

What we know for certain here is that:

Apollos had a through knowledge of scripture
What he taught about Jesus was accurate but incomplete.
He only knew John's Baptism.
He needed more teaching.

We may conjecture that what he lacked was teaching about Jesus baptism and in all the recorded scriptures to this point there is a clear linking between the concept of "Baptism" in the name of Jesus and laying hold of the Spirit. That is conjecture but what is sure is that Apollos was a godly and effective servant of the gospel who was made even more so after his further teaching by Priscilla and Aquila. We could also conjecture that Apollos had known and taught this Ephesian group.

As we explore these scriptures, I am appealing to something that I may call "common sense" theology. It is nearly always possible to seemingly evaporate away any meaning or point of scripture by argument, argument that usually appeals to an *a priory* belief that is held above all others. Let us appeal to some common sense theology here. This is Paul. This is the Paul who wrote Romans, who, in the letter to the Ephesians said:

> *"But because of his great love for us, God, who is rich in mercy, made us alive with Christ even when we were dead in transgressions – it is by grace you have been saved,"* Ephesians 2:5.

Can anyone seriously doubt that as part of Paul's teaching and discipling of this group he was not concerned for their eternal salvation! Of course he was, but to Luke this would be an accepted fact. The question in Luke's mind was not how had the teaching of this group started but how had it finished. The natural question to ask was had they taken hold of the Holy Spirit because this was, to them, the end-point of the journey. What is clear to me from these scriptures is that there is a clear apostolic gospel that originates in John's prophecy, was taught by Jesus, was then commissioned by Jesus and by Jesus the apostles were sent into the world to proclaim it. I have no Biblical evidence that it stopped with them.[84] They, and those that they taught, were to preach that Jesus would Baptise *en* the Holy Spirit, and this was the process of becoming a soldier from having been a sinner. There are stages in this Baptism: conviction, repentance, acceptance and finally equipping. The process does not stop with acceptance of Christ as saviour, essential though that is. The picture that Luke paints for us is one of a journey from sinner

---

[84] We may consider Acts 2:39, to be read in the full context of Peter's meaning. See also footnote 8 in chapter 12.

to soldier and a soldier who is equipped with gifts given him by the Spirit for his or her role.

This was the natural question for Luke to ask. He wanted to show Paul's diligence and to record that the full extent of the apostolic teaching had been give, that they were saved and equipped for their lives to come.

Chapter 10

The Baptism in the Holy Spirit

"I beseech you therefore, brethren, by the mercies of God, that you present your bodies a living sacrifice, holy, acceptable unto God, which is your reasonable service."
Romans 12:1 (KJV)

The development and exploration of what we have observed

* Jesus' teaching that the Spirit had a three-fold ministry, to convict of guilt in regard to sin, of righteousness and of judgement
* The end point of evangelism; it should be spiritual equipping not only salvation
* The Baptism in the Spirit as a transition; a moving from being an enemy of God to being his empowered servant
* Romans 11, a wild branch being grafted into a tree
* What is certain and what is conjecture

In chapter 5 we saw that the Spirit is holy, he cannot be anything else; everything he does is holy. Similarly, in his work he will convict of sin, righteousness and judgement. The picture is of the Holy Spirit whose ministry and work starts when he begins to convict an individual of sin. In this experience the individual will also come under conviction for righteousness and at some point, judgement to come.[85] The work continues as the Spirit brings the person to repentance and then to a saving knowledge of Jesus. At this point the Spirit brings the reassurance of salvation, a conviction that the individual is righteous through Jesus (although it may take many years for the new convert to live in that enlightenment) and a reassurance of the justice of judgement to come. The Baptism finishes when the individual, now born again, is equipped with Spirit given and Spirit empowered gifts.

The Spirit will continue to convict the world of sin, through the ministry of the new believer, demonstrate and empower righteousness and bring assurance that the prince of this world is already judged. The individual is now *en* the Spirit.

> *"When he comes, he will convict the world of guilt in regard to sin and righteousness and judgement: in regard to sin, because men do not believe in me; in regard to righteousness, because I am going to the Father, where you can see me no longer; and in regard to judgement, because the prince of this world now stands condemned,"* John 16:8-11.

---

[85] The Epistle of Jude makes fear of judgement an evangelical point.

The consequence of this is that the end point of our evangelism should not be salvation but Spirit equipping. Traditional evangelical teaching and evangelism has concentrated on the need for re-birth, – that is no less important, in fact essential for Spirit equipping to take place. We should not reduce that emphasis, rather we should add to it. The emphasis in Acts is that the task of missionary work was not to seek to bring people *only* to a saving knowledge of Jesus *but also* to bring them to knowledge of the Holy Spirit's empowering. This empowerment was not just the process of teaching and learning, adapting behaviour and changing ways, valuable though that is, but also the result of an experience with the Holy Spirit.

This experience was such that Paul appeals to it in his letter to the Galatians as proof of his gospel.[86] Now many would say that what Paul appealed to here was the experience of their salvation but his language does not support this. He does not say they should recall the time of their forgiveness but points them to the time that they took hold of the Spirit. An appeal to say that those two moments are synonymous simply ignores the picture given in Acts.

The end point of evangelism should not be salvation but Spirit equipping.

The Baptism in the Spirit encompasses the journey from sinner to empowered saint. A question that has occupied evangelical thinking is "At what point does a sinner become a saint?" When does the sinner receive the "indwelling" Spirit and become a new creation in Christ? It is essential that individuals come to a saving knowledge

[86] Galatians 3:2. *"I would like to learn just one thing from you: Did you receive [lambano] the Spirit by observing the law, or by believing what you heard?"* See chapter 14.

of Christ but also essential that they move on from there to demonstrating and living with Spirit empowered gifts.

It is certain that at the point of an individual being in possession of genuine spiritual gifting he or she is saved.[87] This is not the same as saying that one must have such spiritual gifts to be saved. Having such gifts is the consequence of forgiveness not a pre-requisite. The point is not to bring men and women to a place where they have escaped the wrath of God only but to bring them to a place when they are equipped agents of God. Evangelism should be aimed at this place, not a half way house. Acts clearly shows that this is a process. That the whole journey may need the ministry of different individuals is clear. In Acts 8, Philip preached salvation, Peter and John were the agents of Spirit empowerment. What is abundantly clear is that, from the point of view of the apostles, the job was only half done with Philip. This empowerment is not a secondary add on extra experience, it is part of the whole, the Baptism in the Spirit. The question *"When were you saved?"* may be important, but we should also be asking, "Have you taken hold of the Spirit?"[88] It does not matter whether we know at what point the individual escaped the wrath of God. What matters is that he or she has been convicted of sin, repented, received Jesus and been empowered.[89]

Having Spiritual gifts is the consequence of forgiveness not a pre-requisite.

---

[87] The representation of the conviction of sin, righteousness and judgement to come in the exercise of Spiritual gifting will help to demonstrate whether gifting is from the Spirit, from the flesh or from elsewhere.

[88] Acts 19:2

[89] Acts 19:1-7

So what is the spiritual state of someone who has been convicted of his or her sin and is waiting for spiritual empowerment? The answer to that is transition. They clearly should not be concerned about their eternal destiny because if they have such a concern they are clearly responding to the Spirit and can be assured of Christ's redemption, following their confession of his name and their accepting his offer of salvation. What matters is that they see themselves as in transition. However, they were also in transition from the point at which they were first convicted of sin until the point of repentance and acceptance of Christ although they may not have appreciated that at the time. In the following chapters, we are going to explore what it means to be in the transition period from forgiveness to empowerment. It is important to say that the transition into the stage of empowerment may be slow or sudden, either way, when living in the empowered stage the believer is *still* on a continuing journey towards holiness; I am in no way suggesting that they have arrived at a stage of perfection. I am suggesting that they are living in a place of empowered service.

From an experiential position, that is to say if we see things in the order in which they were experienced, there are different stages to this process. Firstly, there is the experience of becoming a seeker, of being convicted of sin. Next, there is the experience of realising God's forgiveness through Jesus' death and resurrection, and finally there is the end point of moving in the Spirit's empowerment. This empowerment may (and we will discuss this later) begin as a distinct experience but it may not. This is also true for the moment in which we realise that we have been forgiven and accepted by the Father, for some this is a distinct moment in time, for others it is a slowly emerging realisation. The same is true for the moment of first conviction, some can recall it as an instant but for others it was a long process.

As this journey has stages, but is one journey, it becomes natural to preach and teach about it as stages and it seems as if that is what the apostles did. On the day of Pentecost Peter's address set the apostolic gospel.

> *"When the people heard this, they were cut to the heart and said to Peter and the other apostles, 'Brothers, what shall we do?" Peter replied, "Repent and be baptised, every one of you, in the name of Jesus Christ for the forgiveness of your sins. And you will receive the gift of the Holy Spirit. The promise is for you and your children and for all who are far off – for all whom the Lord our God will call,'"* Acts 2:37-39.

What should we do?

"Repent." This can only follow after the Spirit has convicted of sin.

"Be baptised, every one of you, in the name of Jesus Christ for the forgiveness of your sins." This is clearly the salvation message and here is referring to water initiation.

"And you will receive the gift of the Holy Spirit." This could be paraphrased to read, "and you all will be able to take hold of the gift of the Holy Spirit." The stages are the fulfilment of the promise.

> *"The promise is for you and your children and for all who are far off – for all whom the Lord our God will call."* Acts 2:39.

The promise, being the Baptism in the Spirit, is referring to all of these stages, repentance and initiation into the church (signifying salvation) and refers to the gifts of empowerment the Spirit endows. The promise is for all time.

This journey has stages, but is one journey. It is natural to preach and teach about it as stages and it seems as if that is what the apostles did.

There is a commonly held view that the Spirit is "received" at salvation. To this view I would ask for a clear explanation of what, ontologically, this means.[90] It appears to be more about us owning a spirit rather than the Holy Spirit owning us. This teaching follows an anthropology that pictures the human state as having been created tripartite; body, soul, and spirit. This anthropology states that after the fall the spirit died and humanity, both on an individual and corporate level was lost to God. On receiving Christ as saviour the Holy Spirit comes and restores the tripartite state. Verses such as Acts 2:38 and Romans 8:9 are used to support this view although these verses support the explanation offered here just as well.[91]

If we can replace the idea that the important issue, soteriologically, is for the Spirit to fill up a missing space and to move to a picture that relies much more on the shared concept of *en* then I see a picture that is wider.[92] The human state was created *en* harmony and fellowship with God. This fellowship was broken at the fall. God has promised to Baptise us *en* the Spirit which is to re-establish that relationship. The process of re-establishment has three phases. The Spirit convicts the individual of sin as a consequence of his presence slowly being revealed to the individual. The individual comes to a place of choice and either decides to or not to follow the prompting of the Spirit. As the Spirit's leading is followed then a revelation of Christ is given which leads to salvation in the sense

---

[90] "Ontological", see chapter 2.

[91] Romans 8 is considered in chapter 11: "Romans".

[92] "Soteriologically," doctrines that concern salvation.

that the individual is purified from his or her sin. The final stage is one in which the individual and the Spirit begin to work as co-partners so that the individual's life direction becomes Spirit orientated. This is the journey from sinner to server, a journey in which the individual is constantly learning and moving closer to God and come to bear godly fruit.

We may consider the picture in Romans 11 of a wild branch being grafted into a tree. Forgiveness occurs when the grafted branch is set into the tree. Taking hold of the Spirit occurs when the sap of the mother tree starts to move into the graft and the graft bears fruit. That moment in which the new sap starts to flow is that time when often intense, spiritual emotion may be felt.[93]

A problem arises from the concept that there can only be, ontologically, one interaction with the Spirit – the point of salvation. If we see the Baptism of the Spirit as an ongoing experience, the moment when the individual is redeemed may not be so determinable. What is, are the moments of blessing, those times when the Holy Spirit blesses, comforts or empowers. In this picture, the moment of grafting into the tree may not be so discernable, but the rising of the sap may be and will evince the grafting.

Let us briefly look at that time now. Remember we are attempting primarily to observe what we see, not to explain what we see. We are attempting to divide that which is certain from that which is conjecture. I readily concede that much of our adopted theological practice is based on the interpretation of what we see and that may be called conjecture. But where this is so we should endeavour to ensure that our conjecture fits with what we see Biblically and not that what we choose to see fits with our conjecture.

---

[93] For more on this see chapter 14; "Galatians".

That moment in which the new sap starts to flow is that time when often intense spiritual emotion may be felt.

Let us look at the moment of receiving, or taking hold.

Acts 2

Acts 2 is a unique moment and as such may not be a benchmark for other experiences. Nevertheless, when the outpouring of the Spirit occurred it was marked with some noticeable events:

* There was a miraculous, physical manifestation – fire. This appears to mark this event as the return of the Shekinah and to mark it as the event that was prophesised by John
* There were new and unusual manifestations in the disciples; they spoke with unlearned foreign languages
* There was considerable emotion. This may not be surprising. How would you react if you were present at this event?

There is no suggestion in the text that this is what must happen at every outpouring of the Spirit but neither is there a suggestion that it may not!

Acts 8

What we may observe is that:

* After the new converts had been baptised in water it was clear to the apostles that the gift of

the Father had not been fully received.[94] What we must observe is that this was clear to them

* After the laying on of the apostles' hands the Samaritan converts received (took hold of) the Spirit
* That the converts had received the Spirit was evidenced to all, even Simon whose heart was not right before God

What we should carefully note is that this is a description of a group of people, not individuals. It is probably recorded, at least in part, as fulfilment of the commissions to go to Jerusalem, Judea, Samaria, and to the ends of the earth and as such could be a special event, as is the Day of Pentecost. It does not tell us what should happen, only what happened in Samaria. But that this happened, as it did, in Samaria, cannot be ignored. What happened in Samaria would be true to the apostolic teaching and not an exception to it.

On the Day of Pentecost there was considerable emotion. This may not be surprising. How would you react if you were present at this event?

Acts 10

This may be recorded as evidence of the gospel going to the Gentiles, the ends of the earth. What we can be sure of is:

[94] As previously discussed, water Baptism marks the moment in the minds of Philip, Peter and John, that these Samaritans were accepted into the fellowship of the church, and therefore that they were redeemed. It really is very difficult to propose any other view and keep true to the text.

* The Spirit fell onto these Gentiles, unexpectedly, while Peter was speaking
* The evidence for this was that they heard them speaking in tongues and praising God. This is evidence that is observed by others
* We do not have a clear definition in this text of what "speaking in tongues and praising God" means

These events also describe the reactions in a group of people, not individuals. This may also be a special event and as such these manifestations could be unique as this could be seen as the Gentile Pentecost. Even if this was to be true then the process would still follow apostolic teaching and could not be an exception to that. Luke clearly describes what the speaking in tongues was in Acts 2 and he does not here. We may conjecture that Luke expects all his readers to bc familiar with what it means. It is unlikely to be the same as the unusual miracle that occurred on the Day of Pentecost or Luke would be expected to record it as such again. It is more likely to be what his travelling companion and mentor, Paul, describes for us in his letter to the Corinthians. But this is all conjecture. What matters is that although we cannot be sure of what happened, something happened that was observable.

Acts 19

This may be recorded as further fulfilment of the *"to the ends of the earth"* phrase but it is surely impossible to see this event as a unique event. This happened years after the Day of Pentecost and this group cannot be seen as having any national or racial significance at all. What we can be sure of is:

* As in Acts 8 they were firstly baptised in water, which for our purposes assuredly means that they were in a state of forgiveness and acceptance by both God and the church.
* After this baptism Paul laid his hands upon them and the Holy Spirit came on them.
* This was evidenced by them speaking in tongues and prophesying.

Again, a group is described, not individuals. We can assume that this is in keeping with the apostolic gospel. The receiving of the Spirit is separate from the moment of receiving forgiveness. Outward signs in the group evidence the receiving of the Spirit but these signs are not clearly described of defined.

Acts 1:8

> *'He said to them: "It is not for you to know the times or dates the Father has set by his own authority. But you will receive power when the Holy Spirit comes on you; and you will be my witnesses in Jerusalem, and in all Judea and Samaria, and to the ends of the earth,"'* Acts 1:7-8.

What we can say for certain is that when the Spirit comes upon us we will receive power to be witnesses. The exact nature of that power is not made clear in Acts. We will be going on to examine what the nature of this power is by referring to Paul. There are a few things that we can be certain of from Luke.

Luke's expectation is of a three-part work of the Spirit. His report shows us:

* That the apostolic expectation was for the Spirit to fall after receiving forgiveness
* In the accounts that he gives there is some external manifestation that is discernible in the group setting

What we can say for certain is that when the Spirit comes upon us we will receive power to be witnesses. The exact nature of that power is not made clear in Acts.

It is not possible to denote any *particular* manifestation as a sign that the Spirit has fallen.

What is does not show is that every individual will respond in the same way (and, I conjecture, this may well be because the response is individual). Any teaching that says that individuals will always respond in the same way is based on assumption. It is not possible to denote any particular manifestation as a sign that the Spirit has fallen. [95]

[95] Some may also assume this and contend that there is no evidence to the contrary in Luke's writings, in other words there is nothing in Luke that says this is not so. They would be right, there is not but we cannot base our understanding on absence of evidence. Let us make an absurd point; let us say that Jesus was green! Prove to me he was not, there is nothing in the scriptures to deny it! But that is insufficient grounds to propose it.

What we cannot do is to assume that these events are unique, as there is no claim for that. We cannot assume that they are universal either, other than by observing that the three-stage message is universal to every event.

Chapter 11

Romans

***"According to the grace given to us,
we have different gifts."***
Romans 12:6 (HCSB)

* Romans 8 in which we are told that the Spirit is an essential part of the process of salvation

* Romans 12 in which we see the variety of gifts, "spiritual" and "natural" are both from God: gifts are given for the purpose of developing Christ's kingdom

* The lesson from the largest part of Chapter 12 is not about *receiving* gifts but about how they should be exercised

Paul's letters are all written during a period in which the church was growing and extending. Paul played a central role in setting, adapting and proclaiming the apostolic doctrine. Throughout his letters there is teaching about the Holy Spirit. In this book, we are not attempting to address all of Paul's thoughts but to look at the process, in practical terms, by which the new church was equipped.

To do this we will look at selected passages from Romans, 1 Corinthians, Galatians and Ephesians. Romans was written to the church in Rome that Paul had not visited. Paul's intention was to set out his doctrine and to address certain underlying tensions, such as the honour in which the Jewish and Gentile Christians held each other. It is essentially a doctrinal manifesto presented to this key and emerging powerful centre of Christian development. Its further purpose was to prepare the way for Paul to visit and influence this church. 1 Corinthians, on the other hand, was written to a church that Paul knew intimately. One of the main reasons for Paul writing the letter was to correct errors and difficulties that were arising within the Corinthian fellowship.

In Romans, Paul is addressing principles, in 1 Corinthians, he is addressing individuals. In his letter to the Galatians Paul is concerned to defend and re-establish the doctrine of salvation by faith. At the end of this letter, he addresses the consequences of a saving faith. The letter to the Ephesians is different again. Many commentators suggest that this is a general letter written to a group of churches in Asia, that is, modern day Western Turkey. It is the closest that we get to a letter that is written to our local church, in other words, it may be quite legitimate to read the letter to the Ephesian church as if it were written to your church today. Given these contexts, it is hardly surprising that these letters have very different styles, approaches and aims.[96] Their similarities and

[96] Whereas I can fully appreciate the difficulties some have in attributing Ephesians to Paul I feel that these contextual differences, the difference in intention, the differences in the intended readership, Paul's use of scribes and the role of these scribes, provide adequate space in which to accommodate the difficulties.

consistencies lead us into believing that Paul had observed the same process in these very different situations.

Romans 1-11 mainly addresses things that can be known. Romans 12 onwards mainly addresses the daily reality of the challenge of following Jesus. We will briefly consider what Paul says about the Holy Spirit in Romans 8.

We are considering a picture of the Baptism in the Spirit that appears as a pilgrimage, a journey. It starts at the time that the Spirit begins to convict an individual sinner of sin, who may or may not recognise the Spirit at this time. The Spirit takes the individual to a place of encounter with Jesus, showing his redemptive work on the cross. Here, following repentance and the acceptance of forgiveness, condemnation is lost and adoption accepted, I say "accepted" rather than "received" as it is in the realisation of this gift that assurance is taken hold of. So, as Paul says in Romans 8 verses 1-4, there is now no condemnation to those who are in Jesus. The word for "in" is *en* which encourages us to read these verses with the picture of the vine and the branch in our minds.

Paul then contrasts thc dcsircs of those who live according to the flesh, in other words, in an unsaved state, and those who live according to the Spirit; one is life and the other is death. In verse 9 he gives both an assurance and a warning. If thc Spirit of God lives in (*en*) you, you have been rescued from the state of the flesh and are controlled by the Spirit; but if not, you are not Christ's.[97]

We should read these verses with the picture of the branch being *en* the vine: so we are *en* Christ and so is our relationship.

[97] Paul uses "Spirit", "Spirit of God", and "Sprit of Christ" interchangeably here. See chapter 2.

In verses 8:1-11 Paul is mainly showing us the nature of the pilgrim's transformation, from lost and living according to the flesh to saved and living according to the Spirit. From verse 12 he introduces the idea that we are not debtors to the flesh but heirs of Christ.

If the Spirit of God lives in (*en*) you, you have been rescued from the state of the flesh and are controlled by the Spirit.

One of his underlying teachings is to show how the process of our salvation is so much part of the Spirit's work.[98] He is not, in Romans 8, describing the practical working out of his theology. To some extent, he does this from Romans 12 onwards. It is, of course, essential that the pilgrim goes on to live according to the way the Spirit desires. In no way is Paul suggesting that the lives of those who find Christ as Saviour, immediately and completely change so as to live wholly in accordance with the Spirit, which is not our experience; the struggle against sin is a life long crusade. As the Spirit lives *en* the pilgrim, he or she has the *power* to live according to the Spirit. The pilgrim has a choice, to live according to his old nature, the flesh, or according to the Spirit.

We are not debtors to the flesh but heirs of Christ.

At salvation, we are grafted into Christ, we are *en* Christ. *This* is the evidence of our heirdom. As we are *en* Christ we cry *"Abba, Father"* because we are in a partnership with the Spirit in prayer and ministry. There is no indication here that the cry "Abba Father" necessarily occurs at the moment of grafting in, but it does occur subsequent to it.

---

[98] He is also showing how suffering may be part of the pilgrim's walk.

In Romans 12, verses 1-3 are exhortative, verses 4-5 are teaching, verses 6-8 tell us what we should do, and the last, and biggest section, verses 9-21 tell us how we should be:

> *"Therefore, I urge you, brothers, in view of God's mercy, to offer your bodies as living sacrifices, holy and pleasing to God – this is your spiritual act of worship. Do not conform any longer to the pattern of this world, but be transformed by the renewing of your mind. Then you will be able to test and approve what God's will is – his good, pleasing and perfect will. For by the grace given me I say to every one of you: Do not think of yourself more highly than you ought, but rather think of yourself with sober judgement, in accordance with the measure of faith God has given you,"* Romans 12:1-3.

The exhortation centres on the following thoughts: we should sacrificially offer our lives to God; we should leave our old ways and prove God in his ways; we should know ourselves, as before God. Paul urges the Christian to *do* this; there is a sense of will and of effort. These are not qualities that are simply given, they are to be strived for, worked for. Paul urges us, in consideration of God's mercy, to make this our act of worship. If the word *lambano* contains a sense of reaching out and taking these verses contain a sense of motivation and effort.

The next verses bring the teaching that for the body of Christ to flourish we all need to play our part, each part being different but essential.

> *"Just as each of us has one body with many members, and these members do not all have the same function, so in Christ we who are many form one body, and each member belongs to all the others,"* Romans 12:4-5.

Verse 6 opens with the statement that we all have different gifts. God gives these gifts to us for the purpose of developing his kingdom. We are immediately confronted with the tension of *gifts* that are given, not earned or deserved (v 6-8) and the importance of *effort* that is of our own volition and desire (v 1-3). We receive gifts but we must simultaneously strive in humility to grow in God.

> *"We have different gifts (charismata), according to the grace given us. If a man's gift is prophesying, let him use it in proportion to his faith. If it is serving, let him serve; if it is teaching, let him teach; if it is encouraging, let him encourage; if it is contributing to the needs of others, let him give generously; if it is leadership, let him govern diligently; if it is showing mercy, let him do it cheerfully,"* Romans12:6-8.

The gifts that are given are varied. They are not given according to ability but according to God's grace. They vary from the inspirational, such as prophesying, to the functional such as philanthropy, giving generously. Leadership is seen as a spiritual gift, as is encouragement.[99]

---

[99] The exact meaning of all these gifts is open to some interpretation but to claim that they no longer remain the church is tantamount to rewriting scripture. To claim that some remain and not others opens the question as to which remain and which do not and how and who decides which remain.

We all have different gifts. God gives these gifts to us for the purpose of developing his kingdom.

The remaining verses, to verse 21, are mainly an exhortation to *be*. Spiritual gifts are given by God's grace but must be exercised in love. Paul spends more time exhorting the Romans as to the manner of the use of gifts than to the nature of the gifts.

How and when does the pilgrim receive these gifts? Some may be considered as natural, in other words, part of a function of personality, teaching or experience: for example serving, teaching and giving. In fact, all of these gifts, except prophesying, could be seen as natural. It may be that they are natural, some may say that is what Paul meant: that our natural abilities are gifts from God that should be given to him for his service, but this could hardly be said of prophecy, which is included in the same list. It would seem that Paul is implying an extra dimension to natural gifting here, natural gifting yes, but with an extra blessing, a grace gift to empower the natural gift.

After the pilgrim is grafted into the Spirit he or she begins to grow in the gifts that come from that grafting. Natural gifts that were dormant begin to flourish; other abilities are surrendered to God and become empowered by the Spirit. Other inspirational gifts may emerge and be discovered for them to be surrendered into service.

The largest part of chapter 12 is not about *receiving* gifts but about how they should be exercised.

Chapter 12

1 Corinthians 12 and 13

"Now to each one the manifestation of the Spirit is given for the common good."

1 Corinthians 12:7

* The similarity between 1 Corinthians 12 and Romans 12: both deal with gifts of the Spirit, both show the variety of those gifts, both use the workings of the body as an analogy
* Gifting is given to each one who is in Christ
* Gifting is to be used for the benefit of the congregation
* That there is diversity and yet equality of value in the various gifts so there can be no pride in their use
* The most excellent way of using giftings, which is love

Paul spends three chapters in his first letter to the Corinthians focusing on spiritual gifts, 12, 13, and 14. The similarity with Romans 12, both in content and structure, would indicate that he was writing to both churches from a considered viewpoint. We can see similarity with the structure of Romans 12 in that there is teaching, description of gifts, teaching on *the body* and exhortation as to the manner in which giftings should be exercised. Chapter 14 sets the parameters in which exhortative gifts should be used in public: they should build up the church. This should be done in a decent and orderly way and the community in which the church is operating defines what is decent and orderly. There should be a mutual respect for others in the use of these giftings.

> *"Now about spiritual gifts (pneumaticoon), brothers, I do not want you to be ignorant. You know that when you were pagans, somehow or other you were influenced and led astray to mute idols. Therefore I tell you that no one who is speaking by the Spirit of God says, 'Jesus be cursed,' and no one can say, 'Jesus is Lord,' except by the Holy Spirit,"* 1 Corinthians 12:1-3.

Paul does not intend that the Corinthians, or us, be ignorant of these gifts that come from the Spirit. Consistent with our understanding of apostolic teaching he restates the close link between the giving of spiritual gifts and the Lordship of Jesus.

> *"There are different kinds of gifts (charismatoon), but the same Spirit. There are different kinds of service (diakonioon), but the same Lord. There are*

> *different kinds of working (energeematoon), but the same God works all of them in all men. Now to each one the manifestation (phaneroosis) of the Spirit is given for the common good,"* 1 Corinthians 12:4-7.

We should see these verses as stressing the variety and breadth of spiritual equipping. It is almost as if Paul is saying there are so many ways by which the Spirit gifts those who are in Christ they cannot be classified. He gives us two important principles:

* It is the same Spirit at work in all, and to *each one* the manifestation of the Spirit is given. In other words, spiritual gifting is given to each one who is in Christ
* The purpose of these gifts from the Spirit is to bless the congregation

> *"To one there is given through the Spirit the message of wisdom, to another the message of knowledge by means of the same Spirit, to another faith by the same Spirit, to another gifts of healing by that one Spirit, to another miraculous powers, to another prophecy, to another distinguishing between spirits, to another speaking in different kinds of tongues, and to still another the interpretation of tongues. All these are the work of one and the same Spirit, and he gives them to each one, just as he determines,"* 1Corinthians 12:8-11.

These verses should not be read as a limited definitive list of what is available; rather they are examples of the variety of ways by which the Spirit may empower. In verse 11 Paul is repeating one of the points of verse 7, that these spiritual gifts are given to each one, just as the Spirit determines.

The manifestation of the gifts of the Spirit is given to each one. The gifts are given for the benefit of all.

From verse 12 to 27, as in Romans 12, Paul draws our attention to an analogy with the body; only in 1 Corinthians he paints a more graphic picture. His points are easy to see. The giftings that are given are for the common good, just like the way our bodies work. No part of the body can fulfil its purpose, or even survive, without the other parts. Consequently, there can be no room for pride or self-satisfaction with the role that an individual may play in the life of the church. All an individual can do is exercise the giftings that are given and these are given at the determination of the Spirit. Paul does not say that every gift is of equal importance to every other gift in terms of the functioning of the church but he does say that each gift is of equal value in our place and standing before God. Those with the more prominent giftings should be careful not to consider themselves as greater than those with less prominent giftings.

By now it will have become apparent to readers that I consider the picture of the branch being in *en* the vine as being very helpful. Together with the similar illustration in Romans 11 of the wild olive branch being grafted into the cultured tree we have a picture of what it means to be "in the Spirit", "in Christ" and to have the Spirit "in us". The picture of the body, and its similarity to the workings of the gifts of the Spirit, is equally important in helping our understanding of the Baptism in the Spirit. Although, as an illustration, it is not meant to show the journey, that is, the pilgrimage, it shows the destination: that we should be working fully in our allotted role in the body of Christ. It is not God's intention for us to be *only* saved from wrath, but that we should become partners in service, in fact more than partners, we should become essentially part of the body, not only essential to it but also needing the body to maintain our own spiritual existence. Paul gives this picture of the body in each of his teachings concerning spiritual gifts: Romans 12, I Corinthians 12-14 and in Ephesians 4. These ideas were linked in Paul's understanding.[100]

> **Paul uses the picture of the body in each of his writings concerning the use of spiritual gifts.**
>
> **This must show how closely these ideas were linked in Paul's understanding.**

Verses 28 to 31 should be read in the context of the illustration of the body. This body contains apostles, prophets and all sorts of gifts. But we are not all apostles or prophets, neither do we all have the same lesser gifts; for the body to function all the different gifts are needed in their God given proportions.[101] We can desire gifts, and so, by inference, prayerfully seek the gifts that will have the greatest benefit to our local church community.[102]

---

[100] I like to think that Paul and Luke had discussed this, Luke being a physician.

[101] v.23

[102] Which are the greatest gifts? Paul does not say. I suspect that they are the gifts that are needed. What would a church be like that was full of gifted preachers but had no one to welcome on the door? In such a church it may be good to seek to be a preacher but as useful to be gifted in hospitality and welcome newcomers.

In 1 Corinthians 13 Paul leads us into his wonderful chapter on *agape*, love, with the thought that this is the most excellent way. I wonder what Paul thought of those who used spiritual gifts and natural gifts in ways that did not show *agape*. *Agape* is not an option, it is essential, it is the only way for those who want to make Christ known.

Agape is translated into English as “love”. The chapter defines Paul’s meaning; the chapter is not defined by the word that we use to translate *agape*. What I mean is this: Paul is saying that patience and kindliness are the qualities that should be shown when using spiritual giftings. There should be no envy, boasting or pride. There should be no hint of rudeness or self-promotion in Christian ministry and certainly no score settling. Those who minister Christ should be slow to become angry, rather they should always protect, showing trust and encouraging hope in perseverance. These are the qualities of one who is ministering in Holy Spirit led giftings; in fact, this is how we recognise such giftings.[103] I often wish we had the courage to ignore some who give strong spiritual direction but who do not show this attitude of *agape*.

Agape contains the idea of commitment and decision. If I am to show *agape* the source of my decision is my mind; I decide to show *agape* and strive to do so.[104] It is a decision – I will be patient – I will not loose my temper – I will show patience and understanding.

Grace is effective within responsibility, not instead of it. God reads our hearts and our intentions. He knows when we lament our failures and when they hurt us as much as they hurt others. He also

---

[103] Jesus said we would recognise spirituality by its fruit. Matt. 7:16.

[104] Romans 12:2. Although given as an exhortation contains elements of an appeal. Paul is asking his readers to make decisions about commitments and values. Those who would serve Christ must decide to show *agape*, it is an act of the will.

knows when we have compromised and become accustomed to them, relying upon the tolerance of others.

Agape is something that we must decide to do.

In verses 10 and 12 we are reminded that our giftings and all our efforts are imperfect. They will only be needed until that day when perfection comes, and on that day we will see him face to face. Jesus is coming back for his church. Until that day, we will wait and work for him, in our imperfection. [105]

> *"And now these three will stay: faith, hope and agape. But the greatest of these is agape,"*
> 1 Corinthians 13: 13.

---

[105] Some have expressed a sincerely held view that verses 8-10 state that spiritual giftings, in particularly the gift of tongues will pass away at the end of an apostolic age. It is clear that I would disagree with that view. Firstly: it assumes that "when perfection comes" means the end of the apostolic age, for which I can see no reason. The argument that this means the accepting of the Biblical Canon at the end of the 4th Century (or earlier if you prefer) is an assumption. Secondly: if the proposition that *"When perfection comes"* does mean the end of the apostolic age why should it be just tongues and prophecy that disappear, if such a reading of the text is true why not knowledge as well? Thirdly: again, if it is conceded that the time referred to is the end of an apostolic age it is still plain that all the other gifts of the Spirit mentioned throughout Paul's writings have not disappeared, so a case cannot be made that the gifts of the Spirit have ceased. Lastly, these verses read easily and in context if we take Paul to mean that we will continue in our imperfection until *"Perfection comes,"* the return of the Lord. Then we shall fully know even as we are fully known, a claim that cannot be made for the end of an apostolic age. Verse 12 qualifies verse 8 and so Paul clearly defines what he means. *"When perfection comes"* means when Jesus comes back and all will change.

Chapter 13

1 Corinthians 14

There were many problems at Corinth: One problem was the misuse of giftings

* The principles that Paul gives to govern the use of spiritual giftings
* The importance of *agape* with controlled and orderly use
* The purpose of giftings is to build up the faith of others
* The use of tongues

In his letter to the Romans Paul was addressing people he did not know. In his letters to the Corinthian church the opposite is true, these are people that he knows well.[106] Corinth was a lively port town. The church was made up of people of very mixed backgrounds and it is clearly true to say that they were having some

[106] Pick up the story in Acts 18.

problems.[107] These problems were spread over a number of issues. They had written to Paul asking for his guidance in a number of areas, which they had outlined.[108] We ought to take note of this, as the church may not have been as bad as it is sometimes depicted; they had, after all, asked for help, and from Paul. It certainly had difficulties and Paul's confrontations of those difficulties show that they were real issues and not just self-deprecation on behalf of the Corinthians. Nevertheless, they did write to him admitting their difficulties and they did seem to respond to his input (although there are indications that some in the church may not have been too fond of him).

Some of their difficulties related to the way that their meetings were conducted; they had become unruly and disorganised. The purpose of meetings, according to Paul, was to praise and glorify God and to build each other up in the faith. Rather than building each other up, the Corinthians were experiencing meetings that owed as much to personal rivalry and the glorifying of man as to mutual edification. The use of spiritual gifts had become part of this unfortunate set of circumstances. It is not that the presence of these gifts was divisive, the Corinthians had a number of issues in which they were divisive, the use of spiritual giftings just happened to be one of them.[109] Paul uses the issue of spiritual gifting to address the wider issue of *agape*. Paul's solution to the problem is easily stated: do everything from the motivation of *agape*, if you do your desire will be to serve each other and build each other up and there will be no problems.

---

107 *"In the following directives I have no praise for you, for your meetings do more harm than good. In the first place, I hear that when you come together as a church, there are divisions among you, and to some extent I believe it."*
1 Corinthians 11:17-18. There are a number of other references in 1 and 2 Corinthians that show difficulties.

108 1 Corinthians 7:1.

109 1 Corinthians11:17.

Our interest in this chapter stems from the opportunity it gives us to see how spiritual gifts should operate and we can observe the pitfalls that we can fall into if we use them incorrectly.

Our interest in this chapter stems from the opportunity it gives us to see how spiritual gifts should operate.

Paul opens his line of thought by following on from what he has just said about *agape*.

> *"Follow the way of love and desire spiritual gifts (pneumaticoon) eagerly,"*[110] 1 Corinthians 14:1.

We should follow the way of love and seek to use spiritual giftings; this is both and, not either or. Paul has variously described these giftings in chapter 12 (*charismatoon, diakonioon, energeematoon)* and generically covered them by the word *phaneroosis.*[111] In Romans 12 we have seen a different list of such giftings. Paul's use of the word *pneumaticoon* may have much varied significance but it certainly signifies that in Paul's mind these giftings are closely related to working of the Holy Spirit.[112] He uses it in Romans 1:11

---

[110] Paul's comment that they should prefer to seek prophecy in no way suggests that prophecy is not a spiritual gift and is to be preferred instead of spiritual gifts. Rather, he is saying that it is an especially valuable spiritual gift as the rest of the chapter bears out.

[111] Phanerosis (fan-er'-o-sis); exhibition, i.e. (figuratively) expression, (by extension) a bestowment.
For this reason I am using the word *gifting* to describe such manifestations. See previous chapter.

[112] *Pneuma* means spirit.

and in Colossians 1:9 as well as in 1 Corinthians.[113] It would appear self evident that the variety of descriptions shows a variety of function and of use. What is abundantly clear is that these giftings are closely linked with spiritual endowment and given by the Spirit (1 Corinthians 12:11) together with the whole Godhead (same Spirit, same Lord, same God).

We can see spiritual giftings as being many, varied and ultimately unclassifiable.

It is a mistake to consider that spiritual gifting is a concept that Paul confines to 1 Corinthians. It is also there in Romans, Ephesians and peppered over his writings in different guises. The teachings that Paul highlights in 1 Corinthians are the principles by which such giftings are to be used. In order to help our understanding of such giftings it may be helpful to describe them in different groups, according to how we observe them. What is important is to keep in the foremost part of our mind the idea of the body and the parts of it; ideas of hierarchy, importance, greater and lesser, dependency, submission and authority should all be seen in the light of this example. Where would the head be without the feet?

We can see spiritual giftings as being many, varied and ultimately unclassifiable but we can ease the burden of understanding a little. We may consider them as:

* Inspirational: where a message or activity happens following a moment of inspiration from

---

[113] With slight variations in its use it is also used elsewhere in the New estament.

the Holy Spirit; for example, tongues, prophetic utterance, or a word of knowledge

* Personality and character: where a personal trait is used under the Spirit's anointing; for example, serving, leading, or caring

* Abilities: where natural abilities are taken by the Spirit and empowered for service; for example, teachers, pastors and musicians

This list is by no means complete and there is a great deal of cross over but it may help us in our considerations.

It is a mistake to consider that spiritual gifting is a concept that Paul confines to 1 Corinthians.

In the Corinthian church it is fairly clear that the Corinthian Christians were failing in many areas. In 1 Corinthians 14 Paul is addressing the area of their inspirational giftings. The principles that apply here will apply generally so it is very profitable for us to understand these principles.

> *"Follow the way of love and eagerly desire spiritual gifts, especially the gift of prophecy. For anyone who speaks in a tongue glossa does not speak to men but to God. Indeed, no one understands him; he utters mysteries with his spirit. But everyone who prophesies speaks to men for their strengthening,*

> *encouragement and comfort.*[114] *He who speaks in a tongue edifies himself, but he who prophesies edifies the church. I would like every one of you to speak in tongues, but I would rather have you prophesy. He who prophesies is greater than one who speaks in tongues, unless he interprets, so that the church may be edified,"* 1 Corinthians 14:1-5.

Which is the greater, the eye or the little toe?[115] Prophecy is of more use to the church than tongues. But of tongues he says:

"He who speaks in a tongue edifies himself," v4.

"I would like every one of you to speak in tongues, but I would rather have you prophesy," v5.

Some have said that because it is preferable to prophesy they will not speak in tongues. This may risk sounding a little arrogant: do you not need the personal edification that comes from tongues? What does the Spirit call you to do? You may not, of course, be given tongues.

In chapter 13 Paul has laid out the principles for using all spiritual giftings. He now goes on to lay out some practical applications of the principle of *agape*:

- Everything should be done in an orderly way
- Do not offend (and this includes the outsider)
- Prefer one another

---

[114] This helps us define prophecy, it is speaking in a way that strengthens, encourages and comforts – there is no mention here of directing or guiding.

[115] Which would you rather be without? But crush your little toe in the door and see what happens. You might also consider the effect on your balance without it. One part of the body may well be "greater" than another, but all parts are "important".

* The purpose and goal of ministry is to build up the church. If the activity does not build up the church find a way of doing it so that it does build up the church

In these next verses Paul applies these principles:

> *"Now, brothers, if I come to you and speak in tongues, what good will I be to you, unless I bring you some revelation or knowledge or prophecy or word of instruction? Even in the case of lifeless things that make sounds, such as the flute or harp, how will anyone know what tune is being played unless there is a distinction in the notes? Again, if the trumpet does not sound a clear call, who will get ready for battle? So it is with you. Unless you speak intelligible words with your tongue, how will anyone know what you are saying? You will just be speaking into the air. Undoubtedly there are all sorts of languages in the world, yet none of them is without meaning. If then I do not grasp the meaning of what someone is saying, I am a foreigner to the speaker, and he is a foreigner to me. So it is with you. Since you are eager to have spiritual gifts,* ***try to excel in gifts that build up the church,"*** 1 Corinthians 14:6-12.

As we read on let us continue to try and see what Paul says about tongues:

* He thanks God that he uses tongues more than any of them

* He prays and sings "in the Spirit." (In the context, he is clearly referring to tongues.)
* But **in the church** he would rather speak five intelligible words. (Where then does he speak and sing in tongues?)
* There is value in tongues (v. 17 and 4) but it is better to edify the other by letting your thanksgiving be understood.

However:

* He does not forbid speaking in tongues in church but it must be done in a way that builds others up, which means it must be interpreted [116]

- **Everything should be done in an orderly way.**
- **Do not offend (and this includes the outsider).**
- **Prefer one another.**
- **The purpose and goal of ministry is to build up the church.**

"For this reason anyone who speaks in a tongue should pray that he may interpret what he says. For if I pray in a tongue, my spirit prays, but my mind is unfruitful. So what shall I do? I will pray with my spirit, but I will also pray with my mind; I will sing with my spirit, but I will also sing with my mind. If you are praising God with your spirit, how can one

[116] Interpretation of tongues is discussed later in this chapter.

> *who finds himself among those who do not understand say "Amen" to your thanksgiving, since he does not know what you are saying? You may be giving thanks well enough, but the other man is not edified. I thank God that I speak in tongues more than all of you. but in the church I would rather speak five intelligible words to instruct others than ten thousand words in a tongue,"* 1 Corinthains14: 13-19.

Verse 20 says it all:

> *"Brothers, stop thinking like children. In regard to evil be infants, but in your thinking be adults."*

The next verses look at the idea that tongues are a sign to unbelievers. These verses have caused some controversy and it is not within our remit to discuss this issue here as it relates only to tongues.[117]

> *"In the Law it is written: 'Through men of strange tongues and through the lips of foreigners I will*

[117] Briefly, in my personal opinion Paul is referring to the attitude of an unbeliever coming into a meeting. The uncontrolled and unedifying use of tongues, or for that matter any phenomena, will be a sign to the unbeliever that the practitioners are all mad. An orderly and helpful use of tongues will show the presence of the grace of God. (I have often seen tongues used in the prayer for the non-Christian sick with great effect.) If a believer comes to a meeting and hears prophecy that resonates with the believer's heart then that is a sign to the believer of the presence of the Holy Spirit. In vs. 24-25 it is the content of the prophesy that convicts the unbeliever, not prophesy as a sign. An unbeliever would have difficulty recognising it as sign of the Holy Spirit but would have no difficulty in recognising tongues as something unusual. These are interesting points but they do not affect the grounds of the debate.

> *speak to this people, but even then they will not listen to me,' says the Lord. Tongues, then, are a sign, not for believers but for unbelievers; prophecy, however, is for believers, not for unbelievers,"* 1 Corinthians 14: 21-22.

These following verses may set an important precedent: what does Paul consider to be a meeting that is "in order"? The criterion that is set is consistent with his appealing to the standards of *agape*.

> *"So if the whole church comes together and everyone speaks in tongues, and some who do not understand or some unbelievers come in, will they not say that you are out of your mind? But if an unbeliever or someone who does not understand comes in while everybody is prophesying, he will be convinced by all that he is a sinner and will be judged by all, and the secrets of his heart will be laid bare. So he will fall down and worship God, exclaiming, 'God is really among you!'"*
> 1 Corinthians 14:23-25.

What others in their culture expected should have governed whatever license the Corinthians wished to have taken. Anyone walking into their meetings should have been struck by the wisdom of godliness not the excess of phenomena. Our thesis is that these comments by Paul give us principles by which we should govern our own practices today. It would seem to me that if we allow meetings that concern or alienate a reasonable visitor from within our culture we are not acting from *agape* but from the satisfaction of our own desires. Any activity, in my view, should be put to this test, particularly those that do not have any biblical mandate as if this is true of phenomena that are governed by scripture how much more careful should we be with things that are not. In other words, the unbeliever should be blessed by the actions of the church, not confused.

> *"What then shall we say, brothers? When you come together, everyone has a hymn, or a word of instruction, a revelation, a tongue or an interpretation.* ***All of these must be done for the strengthening of the church****. If anyone speaks in a tongue, two or at the most three – should speak, one at a time, and someone must interpret. If there is no interpreter, the speaker should keep quiet in the church and speak to himself and God,"*
> 1 Corinthians 14: 26-28.

The principle is that order and edifying come first, personal spiritual satisfaction should come second (a principle we can apply to any ministry): the benchmark is order and the building up of others.

> *"Two or three prophets should speak, and the others should weigh carefully what is said. And if a revelation comes to someone who is sitting down, the first speaker should stop. For you can all prophesy in turn* ***so that everyone may be instructed and encouraged.*** *The spirits of prophets are subject to the control of prophets. For God is not a God of disorder but of peace. As in all the congregations of the saints,"* 1 Corinthians14: 29-33.

The same principles apply.

What we may note from v 32 is that the control of the prophetic gift is given to those who use it. As we have been seeing throughout these studies there is one Holy Spirit who empowers all these gifts and what is a principle for one will be a principle for all. The Spirit does not overpower us. We have the control. The Spirit does not remove our control or slay us (unless in judgement). We can see this principle operating all the way through the scriptures.

> *"Women should remain silent in the churches. They are not allowed to speak, but must be in submission, as the Law says. If they want to inquire about something, they should ask their own husbands at home; for it is disgraceful for a woman to speak in the church,"* 1 Corinthians14: 34-35.

The issue of women in church is not the subject of these studies so I am not going into this in any detail. For now let me just refer us to 1 Corinthians 11:5.

> *"And every woman who prays or prophesies with her head uncovered dishonours her head – it is just as though her head were shaved."*

It is obvious here that Paul intends women to pray and prophesy in church. The problem that he is addressing in 1 Corinthians 14:34-35 is one of order. "Speak" is clearly a reference to the way or place in which they were speaking not that they were speaking as he has already allowed them to speak when they pray and prophesise.

> *"Did the word of God originate with you? Or are you the only people it has reached? If anybody thinks he is a prophet or spiritually gifted, let him acknowledge that what I am writing to you is the*

> *Lord's command. If he ignores this, he himself will be ignored,"* 1 Corinthians14: 36-38.

The Corinthians appear to be an argumentative lot and Paul is reminding them of his authority in God.

> *"Therefore, my brothers, be eager to prophesy, and do not forbid speaking in tongues. But everything should be done in a fitting and orderly way,"*
> 1 Corinthians 14: 39-40.

This sums everything up. It is clear from these verses that Spiritual gifts can be misused. And it is equally clear that those using them exercise control over them.

As we have been seeing throughout these studies there is one Holy Spirit who empowers all these gifts and what is a principle for one will be a principle for all.

The lessons that apply to the use of tongues and prophecy in this chapter can equally well be applied to all giftings, whether inspirational, personality or ability. All giftings should be used in *agape*. There should be an order in their use that impresses the unbeliever. The motive must always be to build up others.

Tongues

Over the years the issue of tongues has been both confusing and divisive. It should be clear from our considerations so far that tongues are part of the Holy Spirit's giftings. They should not be denigrated neither should they be over emphasised: Paul encourages their use, forbids their censure but insists that everything be done in a way that is orderly and uplifting. I have included a brief few paragraphs on tongues because of the difficulties that have been experienced over the last one hundred years.

Tongues appear to have two ways of being used: privately and publicly.

Publicly

A tongue is given to a congregation. It must then be interpreted by the giver or by someone else so that the body is edified. This must happen in an orderly and fitting way. The church's local community decides what is orderly and fitting (we can draw this conclusion from verses 23-25). There has been much discussion over the last 30 years about the content of interpretation. Some have said that as a tongue is praise, or directed to God, (from v 2) so the interpretation should be. My view on this is that:

* I find the rational for this a little forced; what is praise in this context? A word of encouragement given to the congregation may be done to the praise of God.

* What is required is an interpretation, not a translation. We have the example of the writing on the wall that Daniel translated and then interpreted. The translation was quite brief and the interpretation's length bore no relationship to the length of the original message.

* The purpose of interpretation is to bring a shared understanding and to avoid exclusivity. When used in public with the intention of being interpreted it would seem to me that the criteria should be that God is glorified and the listeners edified. The tongue may well have been directed towards God but the interpretation is to edify not

"translate". I am happy for there to be some cross over between interpretation and prophecy but I respect those who differ on this point.

Privately

Paul encourages the private use of tongues. Those who use tongues edify themselves. Paul prays and sings in the Spirit, which must clearly mean tongues in this context. How tongues edify becomes obvious to all those who use them. I have listed some points below. These are conclusions that I have come to from a mixture of Paul's statements and from experience.

* Tongues teach how to learn to recognise the Spirit's prompting.

* Tongues teach how to learn to control the gift and to recognise when it will be a blessing to others.

* Tongues teach that it is not sufficient to have the gift alone to be a blessing to others; the gift operates as one that builds up the church when used with others as it relies on another interpreting.

* Tongues are a form of prayer and thanksgiving and can be used for such, for example when praying for the sick or into situations in which it is not easy to know what to pray.

Using tongues develops our freedom in worship and praise and as such influences our character.

It appears to me that tongues are a way of learning about the Spirit's empowering. They can be abused (as can all gifts). They are a great blessing when used properly.

Some congregations practice a time of communal private speaking in tongues. This is not a contradiction. I have been in many services in many different cultures and languages when this or something like it occurs. In some cultures it is appropriate to cry out to God. This can be done in the local language and/or in tongues. What matters is the intent. If the practice is part of the communal worship, part of the culture, is edifying and in the control of the leadership it fits well with Paul's principles.

Chapter 14

Galatians

"Since we live by the Spirit, let us keep in step with the Spirit."
Galatians 5:25

* In Romans 11 Paul uses a grafted olive tree as an example
* We are grafted *en* Christ
* We are placed *en* Christ to bear fruit

At the bottom of my garden is an interesting tree. I should say that I did not plant it – that was the privilege of the garden's previous owner. The bottom of my garden is not big but it has a small area that is well populated with a few trees. A little while after I had moved in, during the autumn time, I noticed a few small different fruits lying on the floor. When I looked up into the trees, I could easily identify from which branches they had fallen. To my surprise, when I followed the branches down they appeared to come from the same trunk. In fact, they did come from the same trunk: one tree, two different fruits! A closer inspection of the place that the branches met with the trunk revealed some callous or scarring. What the previous owner had left me was a tree into which branches from another tree had been grafted, giving two fruits for the space of one tree.

In Romans 11 Paul uses such tree grafting as a way of describing the Gentiles' relationship with Israel.[118] It can also help us in our understanding of our relationship with the Holy Spirit.

Trees with great fruits are grafted onto trees with great roots.

It is very common to graft trees and Paul's accurate description shows that he had some knowledge of the process. Readers will have realised that this is not a gardening book but a few gardening explanations will be very enlightening. It is, as I said, common to graft trees. Fruit trees are amongst the most common as are roses; in fact, most roses are a graft. The reason that trees are grafted is as follows.

It is very common to find that trees (like us) do not all have all the best qualities. What I mean is that one may be an excellent fruiter, or bear an excellent flower, but also be susceptible to needing very specific conditions because it has weak roots; the slightest thing upsets it and it goes into a wilt or even worse. It may have an attitude problem and may not bother to bear anything regularly –but when it does, it may give a wonderful result. On the other hand there are others that have strong vigorous roots that will grow in anything in just about any condition, but when they flower or fruit, oh dear! They seem to produce tiny inauspicious little things that

---

[118] Romans 11:16-24.

can often be plentiful but pretty uninspiring. So tree grafting recognises two simple states, there are plants that grow like wildfire but don't produce too much, and there are those who produce what you want but are unable to sustain the effort and are very temperamental. The answer is simple, take the branches of one and attach it to the roots of the other. This is easily done.[119] You cannot attach anything to anything, the results are much better if the two are closely related. What usually happens is that the roots of a vigorous rose have the branches of a good flowering rose attached, or a strong rooting apple tree has the branches of a good fruiting tree joined to it. Sometimes you can mix related fruits, like the one in my garden, which was a cherry and a damson. Paul describes grafting a wild olive (the Gentiles) into a cultivated olive (Israel).

The roots support the shoots.

Now don't get the idea that this is done by cutting down large branches from one and nailing them into the other! It is not. There are many different ways of grafting but what is common to them all is that you need to take an established root, make a cut into it, and insert into the cut some small twiggy shoots from the stock that you wish to grow. There are a number of ways of making the cut and inserting the shoot. After the insertion, it is usual to bind the new shoot in and protect it with various pastes. Next, the graft needs to take. The rootstock has to recognise and receive the new shoot just as much as the new shoot needs to adopt its new trunk, which of course provide its new roots. The shoot will not survive without the nourishment from the sap of the root. A process of joining starts; slowly the two merge into one leaving a scar at the place of the join.

[119] It is easy if you are a skilled gardener!

The sap from the donor tree is given and accepted by the small new twiggy shoot. As time goes on the two become one: the shoot grows and becomes a strong branch, only the scar giving testimony to its past and with time even that may become less prominent. Eventually the grafted in shoot, now a strong branch, will bear fruit. The fruit it bears will be the fruit that it was grown to produce; it bears its own fruit, its strong bountiful fruit, not the fruit of the root tree. But it bears this fruit with all the confidence and strength of the root tree, not with its past weakness and temperament. To produce the best fruit all the time the branch needs the tree and the tree needs the branch. The branch is *en* the tree.

The job of the shoots is to grow into branches that bear the fruit.

And this is a picture of how we come to be *en* the Spirit, *en* God. We can picture a strong full tree with established and firm roots. Such a tree is one of the most immovable of objects; it can bend in the wind yet will stop a travelling truck. This is the body of Christ, called and ordained by the Father. The Spirit is the gardener and the life of the tree. The Spirit goes out into the forest, – a muddy, tangled and confused place where everything competes with everything for the privilege of life itself. From amongst the briers and shrubs he finds a small shoot that he himself selects. He may nurture it for years to bring it to strength or he may take it immediately. He carefully cuts it and shapes the cut end to fit the cut he makes on the tree. The shoot is then bound in its place, a place that was made by wounding the tree specifically and only for that shoot. The shoot is nurtured and cared for as it adopts its new home. The old sap will have to dry out as the new sap begins to flow into it. The shoot will grow from being an adopted twig into a strong branch that moves and sways with the tree, it becomes part of the tree; in fact it is the tree. In time, it will fruit. It will bear fruit that comes from its own being, its own personality, its own identity. Yet the parent tree, making the branch stronger and more vigorous, will nourish the fruit.

The old sap will have to dry out as the new sap begins to flow.

Whose is that fruit? It bears the making and marking of the original shoot, yet it is sustained, maintained, and nourished by the sap of the parent tree. It owes its whole being to the Spirit who sought out its bearing branch when it was a lost shoot, a twig on a weak and inauspicious tree and who nurtured it in that lost state. The Spirit took it and placed it into the scar of the tree that the Spirit made only for that shoot. It was the Spirit who bound it in its place in Christ, the Spirit who supported, led, taught and encouraged it and the Spirit who nourished it. When fruit comes, it is truly the Spirit's fruit. This is the Baptism that Jesus brings, that Jesus provides. The Spirit proceeds from him, going out and seeking the lost, convicting and nurturing them, bringing them from their place of despair and hopelessness, from the place of uncertain presence and a certain lost eternity, to their place in him. When he places them in their home that is Christ he nourishes them, keeps them and protects them, growing them and bringing them to that time when they bring forth fruit, fruit that testifies of Jesus, of the Father, the Son and the Spirit, of the one Holy God. There was a time when they were lost shoots in a forest of rebellion, now they are branches on the tree of life bearing the fruit of his glory. From rebel to royal, from sinner to soldier, from barren to fruiting, this is the journey, the baptism, the baptism *en* the Holy Spirit.

Not all shoots become fruitful branches. Some wither, some are stunted by disease, some simply do not take when grafted, some die when cut from their own roots. But those who are submitted to the Spirit, who trust and obey him, who seek and delight in Christ's teachings become fruitful, bearing different fruit and bearing many times the fruit that they could ever have borne on their own. The branch flowers, and then fruits, the responsibility of the branch is to bear the fruit.

The Baptism in the Spirit is the process by which the Spirit goes and finds a shoot and grafts it into the tree and causes it to fruit.

> *"So I say, live by the Spirit, and you will not gratify the desires of the sinful nature. For the sinful nature desires what is contrary to the Spirit, and the Spirit what is contrary to the sinful nature. They are in conflict with each other, so that you do not do what you want. But if you are led by the Spirit, you are not under law.*
>
> *The acts of the sinful nature are obvious: sexual immorality, impurity and debauchery; idolatry and witchcraft; hatred, discord, jealousy, fits of rage, selfish ambition, dissensions, factions and envy; drunkenness, orgies, and the like. I warn you, as I did before, that those who live like this will not inherit the kingdom of God. But the fruit of the Spirit is love, joy, peace, patience, kindness, goodness, faithfulness, gentleness and self-control. Against such things there is no law. Those who belong to Christ Jesus have crucified the sinful nature with its*

> *passions and desires. Since we live by the Spirit, let us keep in step with the Spirit,"* Galatians 5:16-25.

Galatians contains another theme that relates to the Holy Spirit. In chapter 5 Paul gives us the theme of fruiting. In chapter 3 there is a different motif.

> *"I would like to learn just one thing from you: Did you receive the Spirit by observing the law, or by believing what you heard? Are you so foolish? After beginning with the Spirit, are you now trying to attain your goal by human effort? Have you suffered so much for nothing – if it really was for nothing? Does God give you his Spirit and work miracles among you because you observe the law, or because you believe what you heard?"* Galatians 3:2-5.

Here Paul is questioning the Galatians and is using the apparentness of the Spirit to justify his teaching. There are some important points here but in order to understand them we would benefit from spending a little time examining the situation in which Paul and the Galatian churches found themselves.

Chapter 15

Dispute

"I would like to learn just one thing from you: Did you receive the Spirit by observing the law, or by believing what you heard?"
Galatians 3:2

* Challenge and disagreement in the early church
* Life or death for the gospel
* Paul and Peter confront each other
* Paul is stoned
* Leaders under pressure

It is helpful to have a little knowledge about the circumstances of Paul's letter to the Galatians. What we believe can be divided into three sections: that which is certain, in other words, known; that which we can reasonably and easily conclude from what is known; and what is conjecture or circumstantial. Most theologians will find little difficultly on agreeing about what is certain, although there will always be some differences of opinion. The problem is that the boundary between conjecture and conclusion is somewhat fluid, a little like the edge seashore in a tidal area, exactly where it is, is not too clear; it depends on when and at what you last looked.

We know that Romans was written to the church in Rome that Paul had never visited. It sets out his teachings and was intended to herald his visiting Rome. It is carefully constructed and argued. The letters to the Corinthians were sent to those that Paul knew well. These letters were sent to help clarify certain issues that are mentioned and that were causing some difficulties. The letter to the Galatians was written to answer a major difficulty that had risen in the church. It was written to a group of churches, all of whom had the same problem. The issue was whether salvation by faith was sufficient or did the new believers need to be circumcised as well. It was not a mere theological issue. You could live or die by your stand.

From our position in history it is easy to overlook the importance of the letter to the Galatians. Had this point been lost then the Gospel would have become a Judaist sect. The importance was not lost on Paul who understood fully what was at stake and who had suffered and striven with those who proposed this false teaching since his conversion. To Paul this was a life and death struggle, both for his own life (literally) and that of the Gospel.[120] In the course of his rebuttal, Paul asks the Galatians an interesting and searching question. The question is in Galatians 3:2:

> *"I would like to learn just one thing from you: Did you receive the Spirit by observing the law, or by believing what you heard?"*

---

[120] The story of the first missionary journey to visit the Galatians is in Acts 13-14. On this journey, there were attempts on Paul's life. Once, after being stoned, he was left for dead (Acts 14:19).

Before we consider this, it will be helpful to consider the story that had developed around it under the three headings:

* Certain, in other words stated in the Biblical text
* Conclusions reasonable drawn from the text
* Circumstantial evidence that may frame what we have concluded

Let us outline the story that led to this question, albeit from my perspective.

From our position in history it is easy to overlook the importance of the letter to the Galatians. Had Paul's point been lost then the Gospel would have become a Judaist sect.

This is how I understand the events around Paul's question.

From Paul's experience, two things immediately followed his conversion: the evidence of the power of his ministry and persecution, mainly from his old group, the group that he had abandoned in favour of Christ (CE 33). His life was in danger from this group from the start.[121] He spent three years in Arabia and then was taken to Jerusalem (CE 35).[122] Here he met Barnabas who presented him to the leaders of the church.[123] He preached freely until the brothers sent him back to his home town of Tarsus

[121] Acts 9:20-25.

[122] The chronology of Paul's trips and visits to Jerusalem are not always agreed. I have followed the Chronological Table from F. F. Bruce, *Paul, Apostle of the Free Spirit* (Exeter: The Paternoster Press, 1977), 475. I have used the preset convention of CE (Christian or Common Era) instead of AD.

[123] Acts 9:26, Galatians 1:18.

(southern Turkey) to protect him because of the attacks upon his life (CE 35).[124] The only leaders that he got to know were Peter, and James, the Lord's brother.[125]

Fourteen years later, Paul, now based in Antioch, which today would be near the Turkish Syrian border, went again to Jerusalem with Barnabas and Titus to bring financial aid to the Jerusalem church and to take the opportunity to discuss the teaching that he was giving with the church leaders in Jerusalem (CE 46).[126] Peter was the Apostle to the Jews and James, the Lord's brother, was the leader of the Jerusalem church. Paul's teaching was that salvation, for Jews and Gentiles alike, was by grace accessed through faith. The Gentiles did not have to keep the Jewish Law and certainly not be circumcised, and Jews were free to leave the restraints of the Law and live like Gentiles in regards to the Law. This teaching was endorsed by James, Peter and John, albeit privately.

It would seem that whilst Paul and Barnabas were in Jerusalem they had invited Peter to come up to Antioch, which he duly did, arriving there after Paul and Barnabas had returned (CE 46). The visit was not without incident. Peter had been quite happy to live like a Gentile and keep the unity of the church in Antioch until certain men also arrived from Jerusalem. This group came from those who had split off from the church led by James.[127] They intimidated Peter and even Barnabas who, because they were frightened of them, stopped eating with the Gentiles and withdrew into Jewish customs.

---

[124] Acts 9:26-30.

[125] Galatians.1:18-19.

[126] Galatians 2:1-10. Acts 11:30. "Fourteen years" from his conversion.

[127] Galatians 2:12. *"certain men came from James"*. The Greek word translated as "from" is *apo* which means "away from" or "separated from" and not "of". We could paraphrase this verse as "certain men who had separated away from James came to Antioch."

Paul was made of much sterner stuff and confronted the situation, publicly criticising Peter and calling those who preached and followed such teaching hypocrites.[128]

The Gentiles did not have to keep the Jewish Law and certainly not be circumcised.

We can see then that those of the circumcision group, that is those who were demanding that all Gentile converts be circumcised and that they keep the Jewish laws and customs, were well known to Paul. He had confronted them and those like them many times, both in Samaria, Jerusalem and in Antioch. He had placed his life on the line to confront them. He knew that the life of the gospel and his own life depended upon the defeat of this group.[129]

About CE 47 Paul and Barnabas left Antioch on a missionary journey supported by the church.[130] They travelled to Cyprus and from there to the Turkish mainland. They visited the coastal communities and then moved inland to an area that would today be in south central Turkey, to another town also called Antioch (but not to be confused with the Antioch that was their sending church in Syria). They preached with great effect in this Antioch but were expelled because of fear of the Jews. They continued ministering in the towns nearby seeing great fruit. Paul was stoned in Lystra by the

---

[128] Galatians 2:11.

[129] Paul's teaching was, as we know, finally established, but this group never left him alone and was almost certainly behind his imprisonment in Rome. Paul had once worked for them as a persecutor. They never forgave or forgot his, from their perspective, treachery. It would be a mistake to see them as a distinct organised group. Rather, they represented a culture within Judaism that would raise its head wherever the gospel was preached.

[130] Acts 13:1-3.

Jews and left for dead. He recovered. Paul and Barnabas set up leaders in these new fledgling churches and finally departed for Antioch in Syria, arriving home in about CE 48, the trip having taken about two years. This area of Turkey was part of an area that was both politically and ethnically distinct and known as Galatia.[131]

This was Paul's first missionary journey.[132] He and Barnabas had invested two years of their lives in it and Paul had almost been killed by stoning. They had established a number of new churches in which they had left teaching and leadership. A short time after they had returned to Antioch, maybe only a few months, Paul received news that not all was well. Perhaps it was news that he was half expecting. The Jews of the circumcision group had started to undermine these new churches. They had moved in and begun to teach that the new disciples must be circumcised, thus undoing their reliance on faith for their salvation. This seems to have been a planned and co-ordinated attack as Antioch itself seems to have come under simultaneous pressure from the same group, but it may not have been so organised.[133] Paul would be under enormous pressure. He had to preach for his life in Antioch and simultaneously defend the fledgling churches in Galatia.[134] Antioch

---

[131] It had probably first been settled by tribes coming from France in the third century BCE, hence it was known as Galatia, from Gaul, France. The Romans, who were now in charge, had treated it as a distinct people group.

[132] Acts 13 and 14.

[133] Acts 15:1-2, "Sharp debate" would have, no doubt, been followed by the stoning of Paul and Barnabas if the opportunity arose. It would have been much easier to compromise, as Peter and Barnabas had previously done. Had they done so, the Gospel, as we have it, would have been lost.

[134] Paul literally had to preach to save his life. If the Antioch church supported the Judaisers he would be stoned for heresy as Stephen had been; only a few months before he had been stoned in Lystra for preaching this very Gospel. That time he had survived the stoning, not the usual outcome.

had survived one past attack before but the cost was Paul's public criticism of both Peter and Barnabas. Perhaps the Antioch leaders were not willing to risk this again and the issue was not clear-cut. The Antioch church did not seem to side with Paul immediately and send the Judaisers away. They referred the issue to the ruling of the church in Jerusalem. It maybe that they had sided with Paul, and I expect that this was so, but they looked for a final long-term solution to settle the issue once and for all. In this there was great wisdom but at great risk to Paul. Had the church in Jerusalem done anything other than totally vindicate and support Paul, he was dead.[135] Despite his row with Peter, Paul was content to put his life in the hands of James. Remember also that he had met James on at least two occasions and I am sure had great confidence in him.

Paul had to preach for his life in Antioch and defend the fledgling churches in Galatia.

The news from Galatia came to Paul whilst he was in the middle of this crisis in Antioch on which his own life depended as well as the security of the Gospel. My own belief is that Paul picked up a pen and immediately wrote back, probably returning the message with the messenger who brought the news to him. I suspect he wrote this in a matter of some minutes – he just sat down and wrote it, first draft, sent. It finishes with the plea *"let no one cause me trouble,*

[135] I am not suggesting that the church in Jerusalem would have stoned him. What is apparent is that without their support, he would have been unable to hid and the Judaisers would have caught and stoned him (for example: Acts 23:16, where the church supported Paul in prison). If James had not supported him, the Jerusalem church would have trapped the gospel inside of ritualistic Judaism as circumcision would have been expected for all converts.

for I bear on my body the marks of Jesus."[136] I wonder if he was still in some pain from his injuries from stoning which may only have occurred months previously. The letter was sent back, having within it a reference to James, to whom he was going with his life on the line. This letter is Paul's very heart. It shows his teaching, his pleading, his history, and his pain. It is not eloquently crafted as is Romans or cleverly and inoffensively argued as is 1 and 2 Corinthians. It is almost certainly his first letter or at least the first that we have and as such predates all his others. To put it euphemistically, it was written under duress. And it shows Paul's humanity. You can only love him for it.

I have a picture in my mind of Paul, during this tense time in Antioch, coming to gentle Barnabas, the son of encouragement, his elder and mentor (and this is of course all conjecture).

"It is happening in Galatia as well, I've had a letter. They are in fear for their lives."
"What have you done?"
"Sent a letter back."
"Already?"
"Already."
I think Barnabas paused and waited for a further response. When one was not offered, he continued.
"What did you say?"
"I called them stupid."
I think there would be another pause from Barnabas.
"You have sent this, you can't get it back?"
"It's gone, I did it straight away."
"You didn't want to discuss it first, or at least let someone look it over."

[136] Galatians 6:17.

"I got the message, I responded, I wrote, I sent it. It's gone. That's not all. I insulted the Judaisers. I said that I wished that they would go all the way and castrate themselves."
Another pause from Barnabas.
"Can we chase after it?"
"No, it's gone."

This is all mere conjecture, but I think that Barnabas would have needed all his pastoring skills to help Paul. Next time Paul wrote a letter that was to confront issues he penned 1 Corinthians 13![137]

They went to Jerusalem where James and Peter completely supported Paul, ruling emphatically for all generations and so endorsing the wisdom of the leaders of the Antioch church (CE 49). A document was issued that came from James and Peter and so ended this dispute within the church.[138] One year later Paul went back to the churches in Galatia, no doubt with James and Peter's ruling in hand, and no doubt personally establishing them in love with patience, and face to face, endorsing them in their persecutions.

---

[137] I am not implying the word of God should be different or indeed was a mistake. I am comparing Paul's approach to this problem to his approach in 1 Corinthians 13. I think the Spirit can instruct us through this. We must engage with what Paul says, comparing Galatians 5:12 with Romans 9:1-4. Paul would have completely understood the reasoning and attitude of the Judaisers; he had been of the same view once. I doubt he hated them, in fact I am sure he loved them and only wished for their understanding to be blessed as his had been. The scripture says that it was Paul who wished for the Judaisers to mutilate themselves, this was not the desire of the Holy Spirit.

[138] It did not end the Jews' opposition to Paul who had plenty of other grounds to persecute him. We may also take some advice from this about disputes. Even if my conjectures are dismissed these lessons stand. When in church disputes do not react quickly, share the problem and seek outside counsel. This is what the Antioch church did and we are all blessed by it to this day.

Chapter 16

Experience

"We have different gifts according to the grace given us."
Romans 12:6

* Paul's confidence in the Galatians' experience

* Experience and the Word

* Faith opens the door to the Spirit

* The experience of the journey

* Salvation is part of the Baptism in the Spirit

Whether Paul's epistle to the Galatians was a carefully written composition or a hastily constructed letter written quickly and under duress matters little. What matters are the conditions in which it was written. From Paul's perspective at best it would be a holding operation until he could come in person with a letter from James and Peter to finally conclude the issue, by which time, if his letter was not well received the churches could be severely weakened if not destroyed. At worst, if Paul was not totally supported by James and Peter, or if the Antioch church did not support him, the church was heading for a disastrous split, he would be killed and this letter would be all that there was to defend the true Gospel.

Given the seriousness of the crisis, it would be well for us to ask to what it was that Paul appealed in the Galatians churches. We should recall that he is writing to several churches over quite a large area, so to what he appeals must be common to all. To what does he appeal – intellect, tradition, understanding, or anything else? No, he appeals to their experience.

> *"I would like to learn just one thing from you: Did you receive the Spirit by observing the law, or by believing what you heard?"* Galatians 3:2.

Notwithstanding my conjecture of Paul's pressured circumstances, the epistle is simply and clearly constructed. In the first two chapters, Paul reminds them of his authority and history. In chapters three and four, he reminds them of the correct theology. In the last two chapters, he reminds them of how the Gospel is to be practically lived out. It is at the start of the two chapters that recall them to correct teaching that he asks this pivotal question. The question forms the hub of the whole epistle. This is not a letter of instruction, like Romans, or a teaching opportunity, like 1 Corinthians, it is an appeal. An appeal for these new churches, most only about a year old, to return to his correct teaching and avoid a pernicious pit fall. Paul appeals to their common experience, their experience of the receiving of the Spirit.[139] His thinking went like this, if I may give a paraphrase.

---

[139] The Greek root for received is *lambano*.

"What can you trust in? What are you certain of? What can you believe and hold onto without any doubt? It is that you took hold of the Spirit is it not? You did take hold of the Spirit did you not? Of this you are certain. Now how did you take hold of the Spirit? Was it by faith or by believing the law? It was by faith!"

It is to their certain experience of knowing that they had indeed taken hold of the Spirit to which Paul appeals. On this testimony he places the security of the Gospel, theirs and ours, and his own safety.

What was it in this experience to which he was appealing? It must have been common to all the churches and to each individual. Now someone may say that what he was appealing to was to their knowledge. They might say that these fledgling Christians knew that they had received the Spirit because they had been taught that this was so. But it is the teaching that is under attack!

The Judaisers are saying that the teaching is wrong and that it cannot be believed. Paul is not saying, "You have the Spirit because I taught you so." He is saying, "When you accepted your salvation in Jesus by faith a work was done in you that you can identify, you cannot deny it. This is the proof of the Gospel that I taught you, the Gospel that depends on faith alone."

Faith causes an effect, which leads to experience – three stages. "Teach and then believe" is a two-step process, which Paul is not saying. The implication would then have been that belief must depend upon teaching: in other words, if the teaching changes so must the belief.

Faith opens the door to the Spirit who inter-reacts with the individual, causing an effect.

Faith causes an effect, which leads to experience:

* faith opens the door to the Spirit
* who inter-reacts with the individual
* causing an experience

Paul is claiming a three-stage process.[140] The experience stands alone and does not change if the teaching is changed, as the Spirit did not respond to understanding but to faith. Therefore, the experience is independent of teaching and belief; it is something undeniable that has its own frame of reference.

What we have seen from our study so far is that when the Spirit is taken hold of (received, *lambano*) gifts are given to every individual, in an individualistic way. There appears to be no uniformity in these gifts other than they are given to each one. It may well be that to some the experience that Paul is referring to is knowledge, that is, a deep inner conviction; this conviction is the experience that they had when they received Spiritual gifts. For others the experience may have been emotional and instantaneous. For others it may have been quiet and come a little later. For all, the taking hold of the Spirit is followed by the experience of using the gifts, varied and different though they are.

The point that I am making is that Paul was so certain of this that he placed the future security of both the Gospel and his own life upon it. We can have no greater testimony to the fact that there is an experiential side to receiving (taking hold of) the Spirit.

Is this to say that our teaching and governance should be set by experience? No, not at all! Paul is pointing to a harmony between his apostolic teaching and their experience, not experience *per se,* alone. We would make a big mistake if we were to follow a line that

---

[140] We may ask why faith is formed? John 16:8.

said, “This is my experience and so it must be right and I must trust it.” We must seek to discover what the Spirit has said through the scriptures, our scriptures, and then be assured that Spirit given experience will be in perfect harmony with what the scriptures say. Confidence is when our experience and the word match. When they do not we need to either re-explore our experience or re-explore the scripture. If we find we need to re-explore our understanding of scripture, we should do this with the counsel and guidance of others or else we will be in danger of reading into the scriptures what we want them to say. It is my personal conviction that if we are unable to align experience with the word we should endorse the word and re-examine our experience.

It is my personal conviction that if we are unable to align experience with the word we should endorse the word and re-examine our experience.

Notwithstanding this, it is unwise to underestimate the value of experience. We have looked at our subject so far, the Baptism in the Holy Spirit from an exegetical viewpoint, that is, what we think the scripture says. It will be profitable to briefly consider it from an experiential viewpoint. Here there seems to be one rule, which is that there is no rule, everyone is different. There are, however, certain points of similarity.

The journey from rebel to soldier, which is one way of seeing the Baptism, has three moments or periods of change. Firstly, there is the initial convicting of the individual concerned. I have known individuals who can testify to a period of over fifty years from the time that they first became aware of the Spirit’s prompting to the time that they called upon Jesus for forgiveness. Similarly, there are many who can recognise only a few such minutes: the Spirit prompted them and they responded in complete surrender almost immediately. Secondly, there is the time of accepting forgiveness. Many can point to an exact time and place, often in a church service. Others report that they are aware of a time when they were alienated from Christ and a time subsequent when they were not. They are confident of their redemption but cannot point to an exact time or place when it occurred. There are some, usually from Christian homes, who can never remember not being in fellowship with Christ. Lastly, there is the receiving, or taking hold, of the Spirit in a way that results in the exercising of spiritual gifts. We do not have to look far to find different types of experience. Some individuals seem to follow Acts 8, when the Spirit came after baptism in water; others follow Acts 10, when the Spirit seems to have fallen at the same time as their redemption.

To some the history of their journey would be an experience of salvation, followed by an intense experience of the Spirit. To others this distinction may not be so clear: they may not be so sure of an instant in which they received Christ and even less so of an instant in which they were empowered. What matters is not the history but the out come. Paul's confident assertion is that they will have been empowered in some way, *and that they knew it.*

It is not uncommon for some Christian traditions to teach and to seek for something they call a "second blessing". I can see no problem with this. They are clearly seeking an experiential encounter with the Spirit that leads to edification. The problem arises when this is seen as the only way to encounter the Spirit. This book does not set out to engage with the various teachings that consider the issue of the Baptism of the Spirit, if it were to do so it would need to be much longer. It would seem helpful though to consider this one point. There has been a great deal of debate over the last hundred years around the idea of a "second blessing" and even more so when this experience is called the "Baptism in the

Spirit". In other words, does the Baptism in the Spirit follow salvation? My perspective is that this is the wrong question. We can find a better understanding by asking the question the other way around. We should maybe stop asking when does the Baptism of the Spirit fit into the process of salvation and rather ask when does salvation fit into the process of the Baptism in the Spirit.[141] This solves the "second blessing" question. What is happening is that there are experiences, unique to each individual, of the Spirit that follow salvation and seeking these is to be commended.[142]

---

[141] It is important that this statement is not misquoted. I am not saying that the "Baptism in the Spirit", as understood by many to mean a sequential blessing, is an essential experience for salvation. That is an old and very unfortunate error. What I am saying is that if we consider the Baptism in the Spirit to be the process of cutting the shoot, inserting it into the mother tree, and seeing it bear fruit, then we can see salvation as the moment when the shoot is adopted into the tree. This view avoids the issue of a second blessing. Those who advocate the second blessing experience are calling the receiving of certain demonstrative spiritual gifts "the Baptism in the Holy Spirit". This is incorrect. To seek such spiritual gifts and to receive them from the Holy Spirit is to be commended, but the moment in which they are received is not the Baptism in the Spirit, it is a moment of taking hold of the Spirit's gift.

[142] See the chapters on 1 Corinthians 12-14.

Chapter 17

Ephesians

"To prepare God's people for works of service."
Ephesians 4:12

* The purpose of our calling, that we might be the praise that is due on account of his glory
* Paul's thanksgiving because of the seal of the Spirit
* Leadership gifting

Ephesians is generally accepted as being one of Paul's last letters. It was sent to a geographical area (now in modern Turkey) and Paul may well have sent it with the intention of it being read in different churches. It is a general epistle written to all. It starts with a fanfare of theology, bold and clear. Paul reminds his readers of the major themes of his teaching. He starts by praising and brings into this holiness, predestination, redemption, forgiveness, grace, election and the Lordship of Christ. And why, Paul asks, has God done all this? He resounds with a wall of symphonic theology stating that all this has been done so that we might be for the praise of his glory.

> *"In order that we, who were the first to hope in Christ, might be for the praise of his glory,"* Ephesians 1:12.

Then Paul brings in the ending chord of his fanfare; the completion of the work, the promised Holy Spirit.

> *"And you also were included in Christ when you heard the word of truth, the gospel of your salvation. Having believed, you were marked in him with a seal, the promised Holy Spirit, who is a deposit guaranteeing our inheritance until the redemption of those who are God's possession,"* Ephesians 1:13-14.

That we, who were the first to hope in Christ, might be for the praise of his glory.

For this reason, says Paul, I have not stopped giving thanks for you. For which reason? Having believed, we were marked in him with a seal, the promised Holy Spirit. Paul then prays for those who read his letter, that they (we) may be partakers with the Spirit and so know God better; that we might know the hope into which we have been called. This passage is a celebration of grafting and growing, Paul rejoicing over our grafting and praying for our growing.

Why does Paul give thanks? Because having believed, we were marked in Christ with a seal, the promised Holy Spirit.

In Chapter 2 Paul reminds us of where we were, dead in trespasses and sins. But God made us alive in Christ, and this through grace. We can see Paul's thoughts in this chapter, that we, once a long way off, were brought by the Spirit to the place of salvation. Paul describes us as having been lost, separated from Christ, without hope and in the world. But now, we who were once far away are brought into Christ for a purpose and a reason. That reason is that we might do good works to the praise of his glory, that we might bear fruit.

> *"For we are God's workmanship, created in Christ Jesus to do good works, which God prepared in advance for us to do,"* Ephesians 2:10.

Consequently, we are no longer lost, wild shoots in the world, but we are fellow citizens, grafted into the tree, members of God's household, productive for him. All this is done because of the grace of God, the work of Jesus, and brought into fruition by the Spirit.

God made us alive in Christ and this through grace.

In Chapter 3 Paul reminds his readers that he is still a prisoner. We gain an insight into Paul's attitudes and values in this chapter. Although he was a prisoner, he was able to write the glorious words that he did. He was not bitter or angry, demanding and petitioning God to release him; he accepted his plight as being for the furtherance of the gospel. Rather than call upon them to pray for him, he prays for them. What does he pray? "I pray that out of his glorious riches he may strengthen you with power through his Spirit."[143]

[143] Ephesians 3:16.

In Chapter 4 Paul comes to the main thrust of his letter. This is the point that he wants us to remember:

> *"As a prisoner for the Lord, then, I urge you to live a life worthy of the calling you have received,"* Ephesians 4:1.

He calls upon his authority not only as an apostle and as a great writer, but also as a prisoner. His concern is that they should *live* a life worthy of all that they have received, not just that they should *know* of it. He brings a number of exhortations: that they should be humble, gentle, patient, bearing one another in love; that they should make every effort to keep the unity of the Spirit through peace. We saw these themes in Galatians. Paul goes on to repeat the same teachings that we saw in Romans and 1 Corinthians. He brings his readers to the analogy of the body and its oneness. There is one body, one Spirit, one Lord, one faith, one baptism and one God, "but to each of us grace has been given as Christ apportioned it;" in other words there is a variety of gifts and these gifts are for the building up of the church.[144]

> *"It was he who gave some to be apostles, some to be prophets, some to be evangelists, and some to be pastors and teachers, to prepare God's people for works of service, so that the body of Christ may be built up until we all reach unity in the faith and in the knowledge of the Son of God and become mature, attaining to the whole measure of the fullness of Christ. Then we will no longer be infants, tossed back and forth by the waves, and blown here and there by every wind of teaching and by the cunning*

---

[144] Ephesians 4:7.

> *and craftiness of men in their deceitful scheming. Instead, speaking the truth in love, we will in all things grow up into him who is the Head, that is, Christ. From him the whole body, joined and held together by every supporting ligament, grows and builds itself up in love, as each part does its work. So I tell you this, and insist on it in the Lord, that you must no longer live as the Gentiles do, in the futility of their thinking,"* Ephesians 4:11-17.

The similarities of this passage link it with the passages that we have considered in Romans and 1 Corinthians. Paul brings in the same themes. There is:

* The exhortation to strive for a life style that is close to God
* The picture of unity in diversity, one faith, one God and one baptism
* The statement that to each one of us grace has been given as Christ apportioned it
* The picture of the body
* The exhortation to speak in love

"It was he who gave some to be apostles, some to be prophets, some to be evangelists, and some to be pastors and teachers, to prepare God's people for works of service, so that the body of Christ may be built up." Ephesians 4: 11-12.

These gifts, apostle, prophet, evangelist, pastor and teacher are of a different order to those mentioned in the passages in Romans and 1 Corinthians. They are five role giftings that are needed to form the church and the church is needed to frame the giftings. They are giftings given by Christ through the agency of the Spirit. They come to those who are so appointed when they are *en* the Spirit, grow and remain *en* the Spirit, that is to say Baptised *en* the Spirit. To each one of us Christ has given gifts according to the grace that He has apportioned.[145] Although we have all been given grace to exercise spiritual gifting, some have been given an anointing of grace that prepares others for such giftings. The purpose of these giftings is to build up the church by preparing God's people for works of service.

In most churches today the structure and vision is upside down; a few minister and a multitude receive. Whereas the multitude should minister and the few should be leading and preparing them to minister.

This passage sets the vision of true leadership; it is not to excel, it is to cause others to excel. If a true leader excels, it is in the way that the gift of lifting up and promoting others excels. This is not to say that leaders should not be good at anything, far from it, the best form of leadership is example. It is to say that the *heart* of a leader who is gifted by the Spirit will be for those that he or she influences. These leaders will be seeking for others to grow and to pass them in excellence. No Godly leader would ever be threatened by the gifting of others. He or she would rejoice in that gifting and seek to promote it. Paul is quite clear on this. These gifts are given to prepare others for works of service, not to just do the works of service.

Godly leadership seeks to cause others to excel.

[145] Ephesians 4:7.

In most churches today the structure and vision is upside down; a few minister and a multitude receive. Paul's vision is that the multitude should minister and the multitude should receive, being lead and prepared by the few. This is the point of destination, the fruiting, the empowering, the maturing, the completing; this is the whole point of our calling, that we should be the praise of the glory that is God's. This is not a calling for a few but the calling of us all. How do we do this? By being baptised with the Spirit of God in such a way that shows that he has sought us, saved us, and gifted us. Firstly, he sought us. Then he redeemed us. Then he equipped us. Now he calls us all to live in and show the giftings that we have received and have taken hold. Churches should not be places where the majority come and listen. They should be places where the majority learn to do and to be.

In Chapters 5 and 6 Paul gives practical advice on how we should live. He instructs on what we should do and what we should not do.[146] It is here that Paul reminds us all to be continually filled with the Spirit.

> *"Do not get drunk on wine, which leads to debauchery. Instead, be filled with the Spirit,"* Ephesians 5:18.

Some have drawn attention to the tense Paul uses in these words and have translated these sentiments as "be being filled with the Spirit."

In this book I have endeavoured to show that the Baptism in the Spirit is a three stage process that is completed when the believer

---

[146] Teaching about negatives, what is wrong, is as important as teaching about positives, what is right. This has become unpopular in many aspects of Christian teaching today.

takes hold of the Spirit and enters into spiritual gifting. It would be a momentous mistake to give the impression that this is the end of the process of Spiritual empowering. It is not, it is the beginning. One crop of fruit is followed by another. When the sap begins to rise, it keeps on rising. On receiving and using spiritual gifts the Baptism is complete, the individual is Baptised in the Spirit. However, let us not forget that Baptism is an initiation not a destination. From that time onwards the baptised disciple will enter into a life of continuous filling, of continually seeking empowerment, of continuous growth. Once the olive branch is grafted into the tree, it will need to continue to grow and fruit.

Paul finishes with his picture of a soldier in armour, ready to do battle in the ways of the Spirit. This is a fitting picture. The Baptism of the Spirit is the process by which we are turned from rebels into soldiers. This is God's expectation of us, that we live a life of active gifting and ministry.

> *"And pray in the Spirit on all occasions with all kinds of prayers and requests,"* Ephesians 6:18.

The most essential ingredient to any Spiritual growth is prayer. This is a point that cannot be stressed too strongly. In each of the examples that we have in the scriptures we can see the necessity of prayer in bringing spiritual blessing. Prayer is the exercising and celebration of our relationship with God. If the Greek word for Spirit means breath, then prayer is the act of breathing.

Chapter 18

The Father says, "Put These Gifts in my Church"

- The vision of ministry
- Sticks, fish and loaves
- FAAAT
- Finding and releasing giftings
- Seek inspirational gifts

There are important consequences that follow from our understanding of the Baptism with the Holy Sprit. Not the least is the effect that such an understanding has upon our vision of evangelism and discipling. Our evangelistic crusades and missionary endeavours should aim to leave new converts with an experience of Spirit empowering not just with knowledge of forgiveness: a "decision for Christ" is not enough, valuable though that is.[147] Some modern evangelical crusade strategies would do well by adapting to a church planting model rather than an individual blessing model.[148] The work of the evangelist should include spiritual empowering.

The end point of evangelism is not only redemption but also Spirit empowerment.

Our concept of how a church should be structured and function will be challenged. Churches should be factories, repair shops and workshops for giftings rather than lecture halls and ceremonies where blessing is dispensed. Leadership should not be controlling but releasing: rather than be concerned about controlling the gifting and activity of church members leaders should be concerned to liberate their giftings into service. The purpose of the church leadership gifts in Ephesians 4, apostle, prophet, evangelist, pastor and teacher, is to prepare others for works of service, so that they may build up the body of the church.

Churches should be factories, repair shops and workshops.

---

[147] Acts 14:21-23. The end-point of this mission was the establishment of churches with leadership. We can safely assume that Paul established leadership with people who had received leadership giftings.

[148] Where evangelical crusades take place in the context of a church the important work is the Spirit empowering, the taking hold of the Sprit in such a way as to lead to the commencement of ministry giftings. This may take time. Outreaches need to have long lasting outcomes.

Both outreach and training in discipleship should be aimed at the discovery, releasing, training and use of spiritual gifts and fruit in others. The model of a church in which a small number minister and a large number listen needs to be completely reversed, large numbers should minister whilst small numbers guide them. This will mean a move away from a culture of the excellence of the elite few to a culture of the trials of the common many. This is not to say that we should not strive to be excellent in all that we do: how blessed to be both excellent and many. Nevertheless, a church should aim to have many developing preachers, musicians, administrators, pastors, helpers, prophets, and all the full spectrum of gifting, rather than just a few "excellent" ones.[149] This will inevitably lead to a different set of problems for the church leaders (who will have a lot more mistakes to undo!) but I am contending, this is God's way, that the many should minister not just the few. Ministry is the natural consequence of the Baptism with the Holy Spirit. All who are called to this blessing, in other words, all who are called to Christ are called to ministry. Some may say that the "Ministry" "Laity" divide is inevitable and that I am proposing the removal of thc "Ministry". Not so, I am advocating the removal of the laity.

It is not the Ministry that needs to be abolished but the Laity.

It is clear in the scripture that God calls us to serve him. It is clear that God gives each of us gifts with which to serve him. As God gives us all gifts, he intends us all to use them.

[149] See chapter 19.

These gifts are manifest through our natural abilities and through ministries that are inspirational; but what are natural gifts – they are also from God. As the gifts that we have show through natural and inspirational sources it is clear that each gift is unique to each individual.

When we considered Romans 12, we saw that many gifts are natural, given to God and empowered with (*en*) the Spirit. In 1 Corinthians Paul describes other gifts, mainly inspirational. We have studied the ideas carried by the Greek word *en*. This makes it easier for us to see how these concepts are not *either* inspirational *or* natural but, *en* the Spirit, they are both. Gifts that may be considered as natural become inspirational when submitted to God and gifts that may be considered inspirational become practical when used according to God's direction.

As a young man Moses was educated by the Egyptians, receiving a prince's education. He was also very bright so the education was not wasted. He was sent to the ancient equivalent of our Oxford, Cambridge, Harvard and Yale. He spent forty years using this education. Then he spent forty years living in the desert as a nomad – some experience that! Imagine! Moses had received the best that education could give in both the harshness of real life and in the palaces of kings. Moses knew a lot. There was nothing that life could or had thrown at him that he had not mastered.

Then he met God.

And what did God ask of him – his education, his knowledge, his experience, his ability to survive? No! None of those.

God asked for a stick.

Give God what you have in your hand and let him turn it into a miracle.

Moses came across God in the desert and told him that he, Moses, was to go back and lead the Israelites. God told him what to say. But, says Moses, "How will they know that it is you, God, who has sent me?" God did not say that Moses was to use his natural gifts to describe God and to empower his ministry although Moses was not short of these. God asked for a stick!

Moses answered, *"What if they do not believe me or listen to me and say, 'the LORD did not appear to you'?" Then the Lord said to him, "What is that in your hand?" "A staff," he replied. The Lord said, "Throw it on the ground."*

God asked him for what he had in his hand; nothing complicated or wonderful, only what he had. God turned it into a miracle. [150]

Jesus was faced with five thousand hungry men, besides women and children.
"Feed them!" He said.
"How?" was the reply.
"What have you got?" He asked.
"Five loaves and two fish."
He said, "That will do."
He turned it into a miracle.[151]

When we come to a place in our lives when all that matters is serving God, don't look for great and wonderful things to give him, just give him what you have in your hand and let him turn it into a miracle. There is no gift or ability that is either too big or too small to use and give to God. Take your gifting to the leaders of your church and offer it. You may not see how or where it fits in, but it does. God sent you as you are. Your attitude to your leaders should be something like this.

---

[150] For the whole story see Exodus chapters 2-3.

[151] Matthew 14:14-21.

"Here I am, and I have this gifting. The Father says, 'Put these gifts in my church.' So where do they go?"

The Father says, 'Put these gifts in my church.' So where do they go?

In the appendix to our church constitution, we call attention to the following attributes in ministry: Faithfulness, Ability, Anointing, Availability and Teachability.[152]

Faithful

Those who have Spirit led ministries will have a primary loyalty to the church. They will prioritise affairs in a way that reflects their degree of loyalty to their church responsibilities. They must be steadfast.

Able

What we mean by 'able' is that the individual is showing gifting in the area considered. One would not ask an individual to lead worship on an instrument if they could not play it, however much they may want to! There must be a certain degree of ability. One would expect to find that those who are claiming gifting would show the natural ability in other areas of life.

---

[152] FAAAT.

Anointing

We can hear wonderful musicians who play perfectly but without anointing. The same is true for any servant role. We need to see natural ability surrendered to God, not just natural ability. This anointing shows in the way a gift is used in partnership with God.

Availability

This one is so obvious but is often overlooked. God may give someone a gift and anoint it, but it must be available. To put it simply, the individual must have the dedicated time and desire to fulfil the role. If God does not free this time up in someone's life, then they can only minister in proportion to their available time. Making that time available may need personal administrative gifts. In many cases, God is saying through the lack of time that he does not want that individual in that role yet. Sometimes he is asking them to make the sacrifice elsewhere, give some things up and make the time. Availability is no use without faithfulness and faithfulness is no use without availability.

Teachable

Everyone has something to learn and everyone has something to teach. You cannot be in spirit led ministry unless you can show a teachable spirit.

Let us remember that we are all one body, the body of Christ and each part must play its own role. If one part of the body is sick then the whole is sick. Our purpose, as one body, is to be the praise of his glory.[153]

So how do we discover and release our gifting in God?

* The first question is this, "What is in your hand?"

What are your natural abilities? Can others see these abilities in you? Have you been using these abilities naturally? Do you have a desire to surrender these to God? In your heart, what is your motivation, what do you *want* to do? Listen to the Spirit, he will speak to you through these ways.

* The next question is this, "Can you give this to God?"

Do you have time to serve him in these areas? Are you open to God and others teaching you and challenging you to improve your ministry?

* The third question is this, "Have you invited God into these skills?"

The Holy Spirit will not bring that wonderful Spirit blessing into your ability that turns it into a spiritual gift unless you invite him. Have you given this to God in prayer? Are you expecting his blessing into this area?

---

[153] 1Corinthians. 12:11-31. Ephesians 1: 12.

* Lastly, can you surrender this gift into the body of Christ, into his church? Can you surrender this gift without ownership to his church? Will you remain faithful in its use? As it becomes more important in the life of the church, others will become dependent upon it. Will you still be there giving it?

It can also be helpful to approach church leaders with the question, "What needs to be done?" Compare what needs to be done with what you desire to do and what you can or could do. The Holy Spirit may lead you to your gifting through these circumstances.

As you grow in gifting God may well lead you on into other areas or he may cause you to become an expert in one. Generally, it would appear that God likes to grow specialists.[154] As we get more familiar with our giftings, we get better at it. This is not to say that we only have one area of gifting, often we have more; God is a God of variety. But usually different giftings compliment each other.

Seek to grow in inspirational gifts. These are often used entirely separately from our natural service gifts. Paul wishes that we all spoke in tongues. This gift is the only one that is given specifically to build up the individual who practices the gift. It is always good to develop prophetic gifts and interpretation of tongues. One of the ways that we can develop in these is to become familiar with tongues, which often lead us on to these other gifts.[155] I cannot emphasise enough the importance of true prayer and worship in the receiving of inspirational gifts. Moreover, I have observed that one way of increasing our sensitivity to the Spirit is through gaining

---

[154] Like the organs of the body.

[155] 1 Corinthians.14: 1-5.

experience and through using inspirational gifts.[156] This sensitivity can be important in finding and exploring other gifts of service that the Spirit may develop or bestow.

As we all grow in gifts remember that our task is to glorify God and not ourselves. Our aim is to show Jesus in our lives. All God given gifts used under the Spirit's guidance and control will point to Jesus and not to us. As we work together, we will upset each other and others will undervalue what we do; we are not yet perfect.

> *"If I speak in the tongues of men and of angels, but have not love, I am only a resounding gong or a clanging cymbal. If I have the gift of prophecy and can fathom all mysteries and all knowledge, and if I have a faith that can move mountains, but have not love, I am nothing. If I give all I possess to the poor and surrender my body to the flames, but have not love, I gain nothing. Love is patient, love is kind. It does not envy, it does not boast, it is not proud.*
>
> *It is not rude, it is not self-seeking, it is not easily angered, it keeps no record of wrongs. Love does not delight in evil but rejoices with the truth. It always protects, always trusts, always hopes, always perseveres. Love never fails. But where there are prophecies, they will cease; where there are tongues, they will be stilled; where there is knowledge, it will pass away. For we know in part and we prophesy in part, But when perfection comes, the imperfect disappears. When I was a child, I talked like a child,*

[156] I believe that this is one way in which those who speak in tongues edify themselves. 1Corinthians 14:4.

I thought like a child, I reasoned like a child. When I became a man, I put childish ways behind me.

Now we see but a poor reflection as in a mirror; then we shall see face to face. Now I know in part; then I shall know fully, even as I am fully known. And now these three remain: faith, hope and love. But the greatest of these is love," 1 Corinthians 13:1-13.

Chapter 19

Gifting Shows Jesus

"And pray in the Spirit on all occasions with all kinds of prayers and requests. With this in mind, be alert and always keep on praying for all the saints."
Ephesians. 6:18

* The role of a Christian in church
* Sheep dogs
* The experience of a Christian in church
* The purpose: it is all to point to Jesus

Gifting from the Holy Spirit will show Jesus. An individual who is living a life that is God centred will show Jesus in all that they do. Francis of Assisi said, "Spread the Gospel at all times, and if you must, use words." This is not to say that Christians should aim to live lives that are so attractive in their terms, to those around that they wish to become Christians. Spreading the Gospel is not the same as pleasing the world. This big mistake can lead to Christians following fashion rather than following Jesus: non-Christians do not always find the ways of Christ desirable. Becoming like them is not the path to changing them or winning them. We are called to be like Christ. Some will find this attractive, some repulsive: in Paul's first missionary journey he was both adulated and stoned. It is our task to portray Christ, it is the Holy Spirit's role to convict and call those around us to Christ.

Churches should be ministry factories, workshops and repair shops.

Churches should be ministry factories, workshops and repair shops. A church member, who is mature in Christ, should be engaged in the church through active ministry. Church, in an individual's experience, should be the place and community that he or she is part of where their gifts are fully used, developed, stretched and taught. Church should not be a place where all that individuals do is sing and listen. Individuals should have their lives centred on their gifting and its use in and through the church. Church should not just be a weekend hobby or only a social meeting place. Balanced Christians will be fully engaged in their churches and engaged in the world where they will portray Jesus in their lives. Christians should be in good relationships with their families. We know that 75% of effective evangelism comes through friends and family. Some will have natural evangelistic gifts and will find it easy to bring others into the church; others may find this less easy. We are not all called to be evangelists. One of the reasons why it is important to have a strategy of "volume" rather than "excellence" is so that as many individuals as possible can take on the responsibility of ministry, however unpolished, and be and feel fully committed to the church.[157] If we want commitment, we must promote involvement. It is not good to give church members the task of merely being sheep dogs, people we ask to round up others to come on Sundays to sit at the feet of the elite platform party who dispense the wisdom of God.[158] I have a rather humorous, but also frightful idea, that this approach to evangelism can sometimes seem as if we had a shepherd in the pulpit addressing a congregation full of sheep dogs, all of whom have a watchful beady eye on the one small sheep in the congregation who sits fearful and cowering in the middle, eyeing his captors anxiously and waiting to escape. The sheep-dog-herder (the shepherd) is trying to turn this sheep into another sheep dog. It is perhaps telling that this multitude of sheep dogs have only managed to round up one frightened sheep.

If we want commitment, we must promote involvement.

The church should be a body of people where many individuals work with many different ministries. Those who come new to the church should immediately appreciate that this is a group of people, a team, all of whom have a role. The experience of those who are established in the church should be predominantly one of ministering rather than being ministered to: they should be givers rather than just receivers. The church should have an ambience of activity, where the leaders are dedicated to promoting ministry in others as well as providing the ministry themselves. As I write this I

---

[157] Chapter 18. There is no problem in having a high volume of excellence! The problem is where excellence becomes exclusive.

[158] Of course, I am not suggesting that the wisdom of God is never dispensed from a platform; my own ministry is largely carried by my platform appearances and I am, no doubt, occasionally guilty of this approach.

can sense many of my ministerial colleagues saying, "Yes, and I wish! I've been trying!" To which I would reply that it was never easy. Look at the revival in Acts 8. It did not all happen smoothly. It took some persistence, prayer and waiting before the new converts had confidently taken hold of the Spirit. The twelve in Ephesus in Acts 19 show us a salutary lesson. Remember that this was not Paul's first visit to Ephesus. He had visited before and had left Priscilla and Aquila there yet this small group seems to have been missed.[159] The work of preparing God's people for works of service never ends. Moreover, we will never achieve this Holy Spirit releasing if we keep to church structures that resist the Spirit's working.

We know that 75% of effective evangelism comes through friends and family.

If we look at Romans 12 and 1 Corinthians 12 we can clearly see the following principles at work:

* That the Holy Spirit gives different giftings to different individuals (Romans 12:6)
* That all individuals should expect to receive some such giftings (1Corinthians 12:7,11)
* These giftings are for the building up of the whole church (1Corinthians 12:7, 22-31)[160]
* The giftings are interdependent but like the

---

[159] Acts 18:19-26.

[160] The speaking in tongues for personal edification may be seen as an exception to this rule but remember that the church should enjoy the benefit of such edification showing in the lives of such fortunate individuals.

organs in our bodies different gifts perform different tasks, but all are needed (Romans 12:4-5)

* Gifting develops as faith develops (Romans 12:6)
* Gifting can be used incorrectly (1Corinthians 14:6, 23, 40)
* We are exhorted to develop and grow in gifting, seeking further gifting (1Corinthians 14:1)

The Spirit calls us from the world, convicting us of sin and bringing us through to a place of repentance and the heart cry that *"Jesus is Lord"*. We are grafted into the life of God, as the graft takes and the sap of God rises through our bough, the giftings that we are called to become manifest. We may start our Spirit filled life with some gifting and move on to others but there is a time when we first become empowered *en* the Spirit and move with His insight. For some this may be a process, for others an instant, for us all it is the "seizing", *lambano,* of the Spirit. It may be a quiet gentle moment; it may be so dramatic that others can clearly see its effect. What matters is the service for Jesus that we move into not the manner by which the gift is taken. We are now *en* the Spirit, Baptised into God.

What matters is the use of our gifts and nature of our service, not the manner of our experience when the gifts are endowed.

This whole book is about the work of the Holy Spirit. The fundamental role of the Holy Spirit is to illuminate Jesus. The reason for our gifting is to point others to Jesus and to show the kingdom of God on earth. The Spirit does not desire to be the focus of our attention. His desire is to see Jesus revealed in the hearts and lives of his followers. This is what the gifts are for, to build each other up in Christ. So there is a small discomfort in this book, it is about the Holy Spirit when he is about Jesus. One could suggest that the Spirit would prefer that nothing was written about him at all and that all attention was given to Jesus because this is the purpose of the gifts – to show to the world the nature of Jesus. This book looks at the gifts of the Spirit, the torch, when what matters is what the torch lights up: gifting is to show Christ.

The Holy Spirit illuminates Jesus.

If our gifting is our torch it is the Holy Spirit who holds our hand and shows us where to shine it. He will shine it on Jesus who is our path to the Father. All this comes from the Father's heart. It was the Father who sent the Son, and he, in obedience and love, willingly gave up all to show us how to live, to cover our debts and sins and bring us back to the Father. The Spirit is in the world, convicting, leading, bringing us to Jesus and equipping us to reflect him. This is the love of the One True and Holy God who in his holiness and majesty became that which he abhors, sin, to bring us to him.

> *"And pray in the Spirit on all occasions with all kinds of prayers and requests. With this in mind, be alert and always keep on praying for all the saints,"* Ephesians 6:18.

The Baptism in the Spirit is the end of the beginning of our Spiritual Walk.

Part 2
The Traveller

A metaphysical approach to the Baptism of the Holy Spirit

Chapter 1a

A Little Contemplation

* We can never know all that is around us – to assume that we can is a religion, a Faith

* It follows that we should assume that forces and events that we have no knowledge of, and can never have knowledge of, surround us

Looking out of a small window at a cloudless blue sky whilst drinking coffee it seems hard to conceive that I am actually sitting in an aeroplane, at 30,000 feet, travelling at 500mph. Outside the air supporting this giant, flying container which is bigger than my house, in fact bigger than some streets, is, at minus 40, cold and thin. I can see the riveted silver wing tip, still and unmoving. Only the constant drone of the engines hints at my situation. Nevertheless, I am used to it and the wonder of it has long since been lost to me. Just today though I am left thinking about what I feel and what is real. My senses tell me everything I know, but do they tell me all I need to know?

When I arrive, I am greeted by a cloudless sky. I can look up and see stars without number surrounding the shining moon; I am next to the vastness of space. It is all so quiet and still. Yet, in reality, I am standing on a rocky sphere, hurtling though space at a speed that I cannot comprehend, spinning around and dancing in some sort of pair with the hidden sun. All that is between me, the engulfing X-rays of space, the colliding atomic particles and the unknown, is the thin vapour of atmosphere. My mind and my senses fail to meet.

We depend on our senses. A very highly trained professional said to me the other day, "If I cannot see it or touch it I am not interested." Is she being wise? As you read this, the chances are that you are sitting down. If you look up you will see an object of some sort. Look at it, see its colours, and imagine its texture. To you it is real, an independent object existing on its own. Think a little further. The only information you really have is that your sight tells you that it is there. You do not see the "object"; you sense the object through the medium of your sight. You assume that the real object is what you see but all that you see are reflected light waves, which your sight interprets. Suppose that there is much more to this object. Suppose there are parts of it that your sight does not pick up. Are the parts that you cannot see any less real because you cannot see them? In physics modern "String Theory" suggests that there may be as many as eleven dimensions. If this is so then it is clear that our senses cannot detect them, although they exist.

Consider your sense of touch. You are probably sitting in a chair. It supports you; you can feel it. What you know is that it is made of some hard material. But this "hard material" is only hard to you. Some things, like X-rays, can pass right through it. The chair is, in fact, an organisation of forces. There is a lot of nothing amongst those forces. You are no different. So your sitting in the chair is really one lot of forces repelling another (those which are you and those which are the chair) whilst some forces, like radio waves travel through both you and the chair. The chair is only hard to you because of the nature of your sense of touch and the nature of what makes you.

You may only see part of what there is and only be touching part of what there is. So what is there?

Let us consider ourselves and try to see ourselves as we are. Consider a small space ship travelling through space. This space ship represents your body. Space is what is all around you. This ship has no windows at all; it is sealed up. Inside is a consciousness that although is in the sealed craft has various ways of knowing what is outside. This consciousness represents that which is the conscious *you*. The craft is equipped with five sensors; each sensor produces an effect in the craft. The consciousness can appreciate those effects. One effect, called sight, shows an image inside the craft to the consciousness of what the sight sensor picks up. One screen called touch gives an impression to the consciousness of what the touch sense picks up. The consciousness's reality is totally governed by the efficiency of the five senses.[161]

What I am asking you to imagine is this: I am asking you to consider that a person can be considered to have two constituent parts, a body and a consciousness. The consciousness is within the

[161] Today we would appreciate that we have many more than five senses; for example, we may be considered to have a sense of rhythm, time, balance and others, but for the sake of this example, five is enough. Three dimensions, though, may not be enough. My friend, the highly trained professional, could consider that in physics modern String Theory suggests that there may be up to eleven dimensions; is she wise in considering only the three that her senses can detect?

body and can only know what is going on outside of its body by means of its senses.[162] This Traveller is constituted with two parts. In other words, the space ship is the body and the consciousness. The consciousness is not a little person in a craft. It is our consciousness within our bodies: our consciousness is not another body. *You* are represented by the spacecraft (body) and the consciousness inside (your awareness). The consciousness's only means of knowing what is around the body is through its senses. If the senses do not sense it, we do not know that it is there. We will develop this theme and its limitations as we progress through this study.

The "space" that this traveller passes through is the environment that we are in, some of which we can know and sense, some of which we cannot know or sense.

This "space traveller" (you) is made up of a craft, the body, and a consciousness that is indwelling in the body; these two are separate yet interdependent, they are one yet maybe considered as two. The Traveller's consciousness can ascertain two presentations of the reality in which she exists. There is reality that is reported to her by her senses and that which she cannot sense. Let's call these "sense-reality" and "total-reality." By "sense-reality" I mean, fairly obviously, that which her senses tell her is there. But her senses do not tell her all that is there. What she cannot sense is still there. This un-sensed reality we will call "total-reality". The chair she sits on is within her sense-reality as her senses can report it. X-rays were outside of her ancestors' sense-reality because they had no way of knowing that X-rays existed. They did exist though, and for the Traveller's ancestors X-rays would have been in their total-reality

---

162 This is not the only way of considering the human state and some may not consider it to be the Biblical way, but it is the model that I am using in this book, the defence of which I will slowly explore. 2 Peter 1:13-14.

but not their sense-reality. They are now within the Traveller's sense-reality as there are now machines that can detect X-rays and report their existence in a way in which the Traveller can appreciate. In other words, the machines turn the effects of X-rays into effects that the Traveller's senses can appreciate. The Traveller has no guarantee that there are others things that her senses cannot appreciate. She does not know the extent of total-reality and has no way of knowing if she ever will.

The space that the Traveller's craft is travelling through is total-reality, the craft is her body. What she believes is reality is only her sense-reality.[163] The Traveller is not a little person in a craft. The Traveller is both the craft and the consciousness that the craft carries: the Traveller is a consciousness that is self-aware and is interpreting the sense-reality, making decisions and exercising a free will, and the craft that contains the consciousness.[164] It follows that the only knowledge that the Traveller has of her craft is that which is given to her by her sense-reality, in other words, the sense she has of herself.[165]

---

163 See Immanuel Kant concepts of phenomena and noumena.

164 She is not a little person *in* a craft as the craft is as much the person as is the consciousness.

165 This raises the question of the relationship between the consciousness and the craft, in other words between our consciousness and our bodies. This is a large question, which it is not within the scope of this book to address. It is sufficient to say here that the person of "The Traveller" is both the consciousness and the body, both are equally her and neither can exist without the other. I, the writer and you, the reader, are made up of both a consciousness and a body which can be considered separately to aid our analysis but which are, in reality, indivisible. Theologians and philosophers have been discussing this model years before Rene Descartes wrote his *Meditations* in 1641. For a modern examination see Gilbert Ryle, *The Concept of Mind,* which I mention for the sake of reference, not by way of endorsement or criticism.

So what constitutes total-reality? We know that total-reality contains things that we cannot sense unless we build machines to sense them for us and then to reproduce the reading in a way that our senses can appreciate; like radio waves (and X-rays). These are passing through me as I write; I have no notion of their existence at all. However, I can use clever little machines that sense them and turn the signals into sound waves that I can hear on my radio or pictures made by X-rays that I could see. Now the question is this, how do I know that we have built all the machines that are needed to sense all that is in total-reality? Even then, the way that I appreciate the machines that I build is through my original senses so I have not added to them, only interpreted into them.

Science has successfully described many laws of nature, so well in fact that we are able to predict what will happen in given events. If I knock my computer mouse on the floor then I know it will fall; my knowledge of science tells me that there is a law of gravity. Science today tells us that everything around us is made up of some form of energy: matter (hard stuff), light, heat, radio waves, atoms, parts of atoms, everything. In fact, everything is energy crafted into different forms. Our senses are forms that react to some of those forms. I say "some", as it is clear that our senses do not react to all of those forms as we said above. Are there forms that we can never sense?

It would seem to be an incredible claim to say that our senses and machines can and do pick up all energy forms. The truth is that we can never know what we do not sense. We know that some energy forms can pass through and across others and some cannot; radio waves pass through me but the chair does not. Is it really safe to say that there are no energy forms in total-reality that are as real as my chair but that my senses are unable to detect? If it is reasonable to say that there are such energy forms, then there must be energy forms that truly exist but they are not in my sense-reality. We can never know what is real; we can only interpret what we sense and what we sense is incomplete.[166]

So far, all I have said is standard philosophy and basic science. I am not saying that all philosophers and scientists will necessarily agree with it but I would be very surprised if anyone declared it to be unreasonable.

Let's briefly return to The Traveller. She has a consciousness that is only aware of her sense-reality as she travels through total-reality. She does not know, and cannot know all that is around her. What is around her are energy forms with differing properties but she can never know the extent and form of those energy forms as they do not all react with her sensors.

If the above is orthodox let's move a little bit into the less orthodox, but not too far.

What is energy? We are all made of it; in the physical, it is all that there is. At this point opinion becomes a little more divided but it is safe to say that there is a large respectable and historic body of opinion that says that the existence of energy depends upon consciousness and some who say that energy "is" it just exists independent of all else.[167] Within the body of opinion that believes that energy is sustained by consciousness the big question is whose? As this is a Christian book, I would be safe in assuming that the answer to that question poses little difficulty to my readers. Those who do not have knowledge of the creator God are left with some

---

[166] For the physicists who may read this, I do not know or understand what "dark matter" is; I am just not surprised that it is there. How much else is there that can never come into our sense-reality? We don't know. Dark matter has found its way into our sense-reality though the observation of the behaviour of other elements of the Universe. What else are we missing? The more that we know, the more we will discover that there is more to know.

[167] See chapter 11.

fundamental questions which are really answered by faith as reason is unable to collect enough information (as all the information is not available to the senses). The problem is not removed for those who believe that energy is self-sustaining, how can that ever be known with certainty?

How does The Traveller know that she is not all that there is? Could it be that all those she senses and sees and all of her reality is just the product of her own consciousness, a kind of dream? After thousands of years of philosophising the only certain answer to that question is that she has no evidence to the contrary, only an instinct that may tell her otherwise. Millions of people believe today what they see is all there is. That belief is only a Faith, a religion.[168]

Here is my picture of The Traveller, and of you, and of me. We are like little space ships proceeding through total-reality but only aware of what our sensors can tell us. What is really there is beyond our knowledge and must always be so. It seems that we must make all the decisions of our lives based on incomplete evidence. We are like a deaf man in a concert. To assume that our sensors and our machines are able to inform us about all that there is assumes that there is nothing that our sensors are unable to detect. That is an assumption that is pure and simple unsupported wishful guesswork: a very primitive faith.

[168] To those that say that if they try and be God they soon find out that they are not I would reply that that may well be part of the dream.

Chapter 2a

A Little Religion

* The Traveller cannot get back to God who is outside of her sense-reality. God must come to The Traveller

* God comes to The Traveller as Jesus

This picture of The Traveller should not be too difficult for anyone who is acquainted with just about any of the world's major religions. It is not difficult for a Christian.

Let us consider the nature of sense-reality. Romans 1:20 tells us:

> *"For since the creation of the world God's invisible qualities – his eternal power and divine nature – have been clearly seen, being understood from what has been made, so that men are without excuse."*

From this, I understand that we can learn much about God from honest enquiry into what has been created. "Honest enquiry" includes utilising the disciplines of philosophy and science that sets out to enquire, to ask honest questions, not that which merely sets out to prove another point.

As Christians, we can also appeal to the Bible, which we accept as being, in its original form, trustworthy and authoritative.[169] From these scriptures, we are given the picture of God who exists alone, is self-sufficient and eternal. The total-reality in which The Traveller exists owes its existence to the consciousness of God. This is the Christian view. God holds all things in being. He alone exists outside of his creation. The Traveller senses some of the things that he has made but by no means all. God has made some things that sense the little craft that is The Traveller's body but she, The Traveller, cannot sense all that which senses her. How do I know that whilst I write this a little angel is not sitting on top of my computer pondering me! This seems to me perfectly feasible and well within our understanding of science and reality. The angel would be made of energy crafted in such a way that it did not respond to my natural senses, that is all that is required.

The Traveller's life is her journey through total-reality. She feels that she is guided only by her sense-reality. God holds total-reality in his hands, or mind, or consciousness; total-reality exists because of him. Much of what he created is not available to The Traveller; her sensors do not pick it up. One day The Traveller's little craft will crash, malfunction, or wear out. What happens then? This is one of The Traveller's biggest problems. How she spends her time and steers her craft will be directly influenced by her answer.

---

[169] By "original form", I mean the original Hebrew, Aramaic and Greek texts that were first written.

She can appeal to her sense-reality. In that this is incomplete information, she can have no certainty as to its reliability. She will see people die and see little evidence that their consciousness lives on. She may observe that everything around her seems to be recycled, albeit in a different form: energy is never destroyed, only modified. She may observe that in the reality that she can sense, events that are not dependent upon "will" are predictable. What I mean by that is that scientific laws can predict many outcomes unless there is some will, animal or human, involved.[170] From observation, it would be reasonable to assume that everything she sees is destined to change but not be destroyed. Energy and matter continue. Her body will decompose (re-arrange) but its essential matter will continue. She could reasonably expect that her consciousness should not be an exception to this rule. She could reasonable expect that after her craft crashes, her self-awareness will continue in some form or another, in some different craft with different senses. However, this is hardly certain evidence. What is certain is that if she is to continue her being she will do so outside of her sense-reality; that is to say, in a place that her senses do not register. If she is to know her fate, she must be reached from outside of her sense-reality. God must reach in. This is the Christian message; God reaches in.

We may take a little time now to consider why this state of affairs exists: the state in which God, and total-reality, is hidden from The Traveller who is imprisoned in the incomplete reality that she perceives through her senses. The only source that I am going to

[170] There are some events that can never be fully predictable. Consider the weather. Even with the most complex models and massive computers such an event escapes the predictability that the science of Newton would have expected. Nevertheless, the rules that control the weather are predictable. It is only the degree of variance that allows the result to be unpredictable. This is chaos theory.

appeal to now is the Bible. It gives an explanation that differing races, traditions, ages and generations have found reliable. We would do well to consider it.

Whatever our religious views, it must be self evident to all that The Traveller, and for that matter all of us, are separated from God: none of us have immediate physical contact with him; he is not in our natural sense-reality. According to the Bible it was not always like this. The Bible tells the story of the journey from this lost relationship with God to another, a complete relationship.

The Bible starts with the picture of man and women living in harmony with God who is very much in their sense-reality; they appear to have had evening walks with God and no doubt interesting discussions (Genesis 3:8).[171] Within this story, this relationship between Adam, Eve and God appears to be the one that God intended. This state of reality had conditions. Within Adam and Eves' sense-reality were two specific trees, the Tree of Life and the Tree of Knowledge of Good and Evil. These were two trees amongst many. God told Adam and Eve that they could eat from any tree in the garden, but not from the Tree of Knowledge of Good and Evil or they would die. They ate. They died. The death that followed was not a fall down on the floor and stop working event but a change in their sense-reality. They continued as aware and relating human beings but they lost their contact with God and the Garden of Eden, which was the environment in which they had

[171] I am not going to make any case for or against the literal acceptance of this story. Whether it happened, literally, as written, within the sense-reality that we have today or whether it happened literally within a different sense-reality, that of Adam and Eve at their creation being a sense-reality that existed in a realm that is now part of total-reality but outside of our present ability to sense it, or whether it is allegorical, is not part of the discussion of this book. Many have very strong views on these issues, which I respect. The view I am taking here is that the meaning behind the story can be taken as trustworthy.

existed. Their lives became mortal and God removed the Tree of Life from their sense-reality (Genesis 3:24). Their offspring continued in this new, or fallen, sense-reality, alienated from God. We are all now in this sense-reality.

The Bible ends with a heavenly city in the centre of which stands the Tree of Life. This is clearly a place and time outside of our present sense-reality as there is no light as we know it, illumination comes from the presence of God (Revelation 21:23). This city contains the nations. The dwelling of God is with humanity in this city. They are his people and God himself is with them, living with them, (Revelation 21-22).

The Bible story is the story of this journey, from Eden, through our present sense-reality, to the new heaven and new earth where God once again dwells in full communion with us. However, there is more to this eternal reality than the city. There is also the lake of fire into which those whose names were not found in the book of life where thrown (Revelation 20).[172] The Bible story ends in Revelation with two destinies: one is the full presence and joy of God; the other is total alienation from God, described as the lake of fire.

The story of the Garden of Eden tells us why this is so. To today's minds, the explanation may not seem sufficient but it is the explanation that God has given to us and as such we cannot improve upon it. We are separated from God. Earlier we considered our ability to know who and what we are. We saw that it is as much

[172] There are many strongly held views about the nature of the lake of fire and the city. I am not going to enter into them. I am only saying that these places, whatever they are, are the end point of the Bible story and as such can be taken as trustworthy. Jesus talked about such a division calling one his Father's house and the other the city garbage tip.

a state of faith to believe that there is no God as to believe that there is a God; in fact we need some intuitive knowledge to decide that we are not God. When Adam and Eve rebelled against God in the Garden, they were put out of the Garden and the presence of God and into the sense-reality of today.[173] Everything that they (we) now appreciate is different from how Adam and Eve sensed it. We are the generations that were born into this sense-reality, a fallen reality, not appreciating God.

The question that the Bible asks is, “Do we want to get back to God?”, and if we do it tells us how.

If The Traveller does not wish to fellowship with God then she does not need to do anything as she is already in that state. We will look at the consequences of this a little later. If she wants fellowship with God, there are a few considerations.

The way back to God will, in some way, involve changing our sense-reality. It may be possible to have an understanding of the presence of God with our existing equipment but to be in anything like the original fellowship would clearly mean a major change.[174] Thousands of years of written history have shown us that we are not able to do this. If we are to re-gain any fellowship with God, God must come to us, as we have not been able to go to him. This is one of the messages of the Bible.

---

[173] In Eden, Adam and Eve could appreciate God with their senses. Now we cannot. God does not change so it must be that our senses have changed, we cannot appreciate the presence of God and meet with him. We must therefore be in a different sense-reality.

[174] Philippians 3:20-21 indicates the nature of a new heavenly body and a new body must infer new senses.

Because of Adam's disobedience, death came to all humanity: from Adam on, we are all born in a sense-reality that cannot sense God. God has redressed the balance by sending a man through whose obedience a way is made back to him. This man is not just an ordinary man but the man that God is.[175] Jesus came into our sense-reality and showed us how to live. The people around him at the time did not like this and killed him. We should be careful if we think that we would have done any different. Nevertheless, God raised him from the dead to show that he had the authority to redress the effects of Adam's death. The Apostle Paul describes the problem like this.

For since death came through a man, the resurrection of the dead comes also through a man.

> *"For as in Adam all die, so in Christ all will be made alive,"* 1 Corinthians 15:21-22.

[175] The idea of God becoming a man has caused problems to many. But if God is the eternal creator he can do anything and what may seem difficult to us is not for him. Jesus was fully God and fully man.

Chapter 3a

A Little Explanation

* Sin is the theological word for Adam and Eves' rebellion. This rebellion changed their sense-reality and the sense-reality of all who followed them. This is the problem

* God did something about it, he came as Jesus whose life, death and resurrection is the way to solve the problem

* To accept this solution we need to respond

Christ's life, death and resurrection are to do with the Biblical concept of sin.

The revelation of the nature of God is interwoven with the Biblical story of humanity's reconciliation with God; it is an integral part of the story. Throughout the Bible, starting with Genesis and running throughout the whole of the Old Testament, restated in the New Testament and graphically shown in Revelation, is the picture of

God who is both just and compassionate; a God who both punishes the wicked and shows forgiveness to those who seek him. The Bible is a collection of writings given over a period of thousands of years into very different cultures in three different languages. If we are true to its big picture, we cannot avoid the issue of God's anger. The result of Adam and Eves' rebellion was to cause God to be angry. To try to avoid this issue, or to try to restate it in a way that is more acceptable to modern thinking is to ignore what the Bible actually says. It is true that the Bible was written to ancient cultures and that our own view of our perceived rights and our view of our place and status in our time has moved since it was first written: the prevailing western attitude today is that we are above judgement. This does not invalidate the Bible's teaching. We are just one culture flourishing in one time; the Bible is written to all cultures in all times. God has a response to Adam and Eves' rebellion; it is a response that contains both anger and compassion.

Sin is the theological word for Adam and Eves' rebellion. This rebellion changed their sense-reality and the sense-reality of all who followed them. The Bible says that we all exist in a state of sin, a state that God did not desire but one that has been caused by that rebellion. We all live in the consequence, alienation from God. What does God feel about this? Quite a lot, he is angry. His anger is directed to those who follow Adam and Eve for no other reason than they are content to stay in this condition and in accepting it, they also accept their identification and responsibility with Adam and Eve for the initial transgression.

"But," someone may object, "I want to get back to God." Then you will.[176] God has made a way back; a way in which he comes to us and we need to respond. God became a man, Jesus. He lived an

---

[176] This is not to say that you can get back to a "god" of your own making or design.

exemplary life. He was never in the state of sin that entered the world with Adam and Eve as he is both God and man; God was in Jesus sense-reality. On the cross Jesus died not just a human death but also a death that reversed the death of Adam. His death satisfied God's anger and opened the way for the error of sin to be reversed. Jesus' raising from the dead is the proof that God is pleased and satisfied.

The Bible has much to say about all this, both about the reasons for Christ's death and the importance of the resurrection, but, important as these issues are, they are not the subject of our discussions. Rather than discuss and explore them I am just going to state what the Bible teaches.

There is a problem

* We are all under sin
* Sin has eternal penalties, notably alienation from God
* God is angered by this state of affairs.

God did something about it

* He came to us in the form of a man
* Jesus died on the cross and then rose from the dead
* His death and resurrection satisfied God's need for justice and God's demand that a penalty be paid.

We need to respond

* Those who accept that Jesus' death and resurrection are the only grounds for their way

back to God will be counted by God as being forgiven

* An essential part of this response is to confess our state of sin, to confess the things that we have done that are contrary to God's laws, and ask for God's forgiveness.

If we reject God's way we will remain in our state of sin. We cannot change our sense-reality and get back to God on our own.

When and how does this happen? These are the questions that we are addressing. Let us turn our thoughts to The Traveller. She is both a consciousness and a craft. The Bible teaches us that when the craft crashes the consciousness carries on in a new sense-reality (in a resurrection craft). Those who accept the salvation message will find their consciousness will inherit the heavenly city. Those who reject God's salvation through Jesus whilst in their craft, will find that after the craft has crashed their consciousness in their new sense-reality will not inherit the heavenly city; they have rejected God and have chosen the lake of fire.

God is angry at the initial transgression and angry with those who reject his way back.

Jesus explained it like this:

> *"For God so loved the world that he gave his one and only Son, [Jesus] that whoever believes in him shall not perish but have eternal life. For God did not send his Son into the world to condemn the world, but to save the world through him. Whoever believes in him is not condemned, but whoever does not believe stands condemned already because he has not believed in the name of God's one and only Son.*

> *This is the verdict: Light has come into the world, but men loved darkness instead of light because their deeds were evil. Everyone who does evil hates the light, and will not come into the light for fear that his deeds will be exposed. But whoever lives by the truth comes into the light, so that it may be seen plainly that what he has done has been done through God,"* John 3:16-21.

These famous words of Jesus should be read carefully. Jesus is pointing out two paths. There are *"those who believe in him"* who will not perish but *"have eternal life."* There are those who do not believe who *"stands condemned already because he has not believed in the name of God's one and only Son."* Because their deeds are evil they hate the Light of God and reject him. This rejection is the same as Adam and Eves'.

Paul says this in 2 Thessalonians 1:8-9:

> *"He will punish those who do not know God and do not obey the gospel of our Lord Jesus. They will be punished with everlasting destruction and shut out from the presence of the Lord and from the majesty of his power."*

It is respectable today to ask the question of God, "Just who does he think he is to make and have such demands?" to which the answer is rather obvious – God. We are human, a part of his creation, our lives and bodies and consciousness are given to us by him, and this is how it is. It is not that God does not have any respect or concern for us. God became the object of his own wrath to find a way to bring us back to him that is acceptable to him in his eternal reality. He demanded a penalty for sin and for the continual sinful rebellion. This is his justice. In his love he subjected himself to his own demands and he suffered punishment for us. This is what we mean by God's love for us.

Since we have adopted Adam and Eves' sin, continued in their rebellion, and rejected God's own salvation through Jesus' life and death, why is it that God bothers with us at all? It is not because we are worth it. It is because of God's nature. This side of God's nature we give a specific theological term to, we call it grace.

So, to summarise, what do we learn from the Bible about our state and position with God today? We are separated from God and identified with Adam and Eves' initial sin; the Bible says we are all sinners. If anyone doubts this all they have to do is to appeal to their experience; are they in sense contact with God, and do they, by nature, do things that are not approved of by God?

There are two consequences from this state, lack of fellowship with God in this life and alienation from God in the next. To reverse this state God became man, the man Jesus. His life is our example and his death and resurrection open the way for our forgiveness. Forgiveness results in fellowship with God in this life (but not sense recognition) and eternal fellowship with God in the next life with sense recognition.

The Bible gives a number of pictures to explain how this occurs and why it needs to occur. One is the picture of a slave in a slave market who is owned by "sin." God desires to purchase the slave, his motive being his own love and grace. To purchase, or redeem, the slave a price has to be set. In order to pay a price that would be high enough to purchase all that sin owns and to show his inexhaustible grace, God offers the infinite price, himself, and dies in the death of Jesus, to provide such a price. Another picture is that of the Old Testament sacrifices. Here God says that for sin to be forgiven there needs to be a sacrifice of life; life was lost in Eden and to purchase life back life must be given. In the Old Testament this was done by animal sacrifice. When Jesus died, the ultimate had died and the ultimate sacrifice had been made. As the ultimate price has been paid there is no need for any other price or any other sacrifice. [177]

Here is the problem; we are alienated from God and to come back to God demands a price. Here is the solution; Jesus paid that price. To receive the benefit we need to accept the offer.

> *"In the past God spoke to our forefathers through the prophets at many times and in various ways. But in these last days he has spoken to us by his Son, whom he appointed heir of all things, and through whom he made the universe. The Son is the radiance of God's glory and the exact representation of his being, sustaining all things by his powerful word. After he had provided purification for sins, he sat down at the right hand of the Majesty in heaven,"* Hebrews 1:1-3.

[177] These pictures do not always register with us as they would have done to previous societies but they are the teaching that God gives us. One question that is asked today goes like this. Did Christ die and rise from the dead to satisfy God's previously existing demands or are the demands and prophecies there to point to and explain his death and resurrection? In other words, which came first in God's planning, the demands of the Law and the prophecies, or Christ's death and resurrection? This book does not discuss this, I raise it for completeness although readers may sense that I tend towards the belief that Christ's death and resurrection came first in God's planning.

Chapter 4a

A Little Common Sense

* Instinct
* Our internal knowledge
* Why don't we consider the question that asks, "Are you God?"

"By the word of the LORD were the heavens made, their starry host by the breath of his mouth. He gathers the waters of the sea into jars; he puts the deep into storehouses. Let all the earth fear the LORD; let all the people of the world revere him. For he spoke, and it came to be; he commanded, and it stood firm," Psalm 33:6-9.

"The Son is the radiance of God's glory and the exact representation of his being, sustaining all things by his powerful word. After he had provided purification for sins, he sat down at the right hand of the Majesty in heaven," Hebrews 1:3.

Let's turn our attention to The Traveller again. She is constituted by two factors: that which she can demonstrate is made up of physical forces; and that which she experiences but she is unable to be certain of what constitutes it, in other words, her body and consciousness.[178] A Christian perspective puts her into a context with God. God is the pre-existing self-aware eternal consciousness who holds all things in being. God has created The Traveller in such a way as to give her a free will.[179] As such, her decisions and the decisions of others affect her. The Traveller has only a limited knowledge of what God has created and who and what God is. She can collect the information that God has made available to her through her senses and we have been calling the world that she sees and knows through these senses the world of her sense-reality.

God's creating consciousness provides total-reality and he is present in all of total-reality.[180] God's existence is not supported by total-reality; he *created* and continues to maintain total-reality. He exists as himself, eternal, timeless, and spaceless; he created time and space and so can exist without and out side of them. The Traveller can recognise the existence of three realities: her reality, which is her sense-reality; total-reality, which is her sense-reality and all else that she cannot perceive, some of which she will never perceive; and God. God's reality is himself. He existed and may exists outside of all that he created and maintains, and all that there is outside of what he has created is himself. He self-exists; he is self-sufficient. The Traveller is like a small spacecraft that travels

---

[178] See footnote 2 chapter 1.

[179] There are some who dispute that she has a free will. The perspective that I am coming from accepts that from both a Biblical and philosophical view The Traveller has a measure of self-determination within the limits of her natural powers.

[180] Jeremiah 23:23-24.

through total-reality, her senses telling her something about total-reality but not everything. One of The Traveller's problems is finding ways by which she can be certain of what she knows. At this point of our exploration, we have tended to infer that all she knows comes through her senses, but is this true? Does she have other ways of attaining trustworthy knowledge? I think so.

A few years ago, I was privileged to be on holiday in Florida visiting family. My nephew, an employee of the State of Florida, told us that we were there at the time that the big turtles come out of the sea and lay their eggs in the sand. I very much wanted to see this so after giving me all the do's and don'ts and all the ecological and environmental codes; instructing me as to the local laws; telling me where and when I may go and particularly telling me that I was not to disturb any turtle I may come across; after ensuring that I was familiar with all that he had told me, he instructed me as to when, where and which part of the beach I should walk up and down (without a torch in the dark in case I disturbed any turtles). My daughter came with me and after walking miles and providing mosquitoes the size of bats with free meals we were rewarded. We saw a large turtle dragging herself up the beach, digging a huge hole, laying her eggs, burying them again and dragging herself down the beach into the welcoming sea.

We had, unfortunately, left Florida by the time the eggs hatched out as it would have appealed very much to my sense of wonder to have been present when the little turtles hatched out, dug their way up, flip flopped their way down the beach and entered the surf.

How do you get into the mind of a turtle? How does it do it? How does the baby turtle do it?! There it is, buried, way down in the sand and it knows what to do. It somehow knows when to start sawing its way thorough its shell. Then with an option to go in any direction in the dark sand, it knows it has to go up. Why not down or side ways?

But no, it knows it has to go up. Then it calmly takes a bearing and heads off to the sea. How does it know that that is what it needs to do, why not head up the beach into the grass? It knows how to saw, dig, "walk," and then swim, and it knows in which direction to swim and the necessary manner of its swimming (out, quickly!). How does it know how to do all this?

Sometimes I fear that our modern knowledge causes us to lose the pleasure of wonderment. Most of this can and has been explained. It all comes down to genes, DNA and encrypted chemical codes. The little turtle is simply following pre-programmed instructions. We are all in receipt of such codes and directions.

No one tells a baby how to suckle or the mother to care. No one tells the child to trust its parents. We just do, we are genetically programmed. We are not born as blank slates with nothing written on them; we are born with a wealth of instincts and directions. The Traveller can access these and learn from them. She can learn of her instincts to love, and also see evidence of the sinful state that she is in by her readiness to hate. Much of The Traveller's attitudes and skills will be rooted in this genetic programming. We may appreciate that the gap between her consciousness and her craft may not be as great and as distinct as it first appears.

Such knowledge does no directly report on The Traveller's appreciation of total-reality but it is part of the process by which she handles the information that she does have. She may make assumptions from it concerning the nature of God and of herself. It is important and is very much part of The Traveller. It is largely responsible for the size and nature and shape of her craft, setting much of its potential and direction. It affects how she handles what she sees, it is part of the process by which she understands what she sees. It may contribute to the nature of her attitudes.

The little turtle "knew" what the beach was and what the sea means to it. This knowledge was much more powerful and important to it than anything else at its first moments. It may be so with us and we may, as we get older, overrule our genetic predisposition to a greater or lesser extent. I am not going to consider this aspect of The Traveller again but we need to acknowledge the importance and the presence of such information.

There is another source of reliable information that The Traveller has available to her that does tell her about total-reality, albeit controversial. In order to explore it let me take one scenario.

In the first episode of our story about The Traveller we asked how it was that The Traveller does not know that she is all that there is. This is a very reasonable question. The more familiar we become with something the less wonderful it seems. Let's focus on The Traveller (and you and me) for a moment. The Traveller is truly confident of her own awareness; she knows that she exists because she is aware of herself.[181] She is aware of what it means to dream and has had dreams in which she thought she was in reality, only to wake and find that she was not. So what of now, is she going to wake and find that this is not reality? Is she, The Traveller (or you or me), the only consciousness; is she "God"? (Or, to put it more poignantly, how do you know that you are not God?) [182] Attempts to refute this argument by pointing to our powerlessness to change our destiny through our will, will only draw comparisons with our dream states in which we surely all have had dreams in which we have tried to change our destiny but been unable to. The Traveller would need good evidence to be convinced that she is not the only consciousness in existence, that everything and everybody else was

[181] A teaching better known its original form "*Cogito, ergo sum*" – I think therefore I am. René Descartes 1637

[182] By "God" in this context, I mean the only consciousness that exists.

not just figments of her creativity. How does she know that she is not God? There are many scenarios that we could imagine – that God is alone and has created a world that he accesses through being The Traveller and when The Traveller wakes up God will create for himself another dream. We may have many debates about the nature of such a God, but that is not the point at issue.[183] These scenarios may seem far-fetched but let us return to the facts, the only fact that The Traveller has is that she is. The Traveller would need good information to discount completely the possibility that she is alone. And there are many philosophical discussions and "proofs" to show that The Traveller is not alone, all, in my humble opinion, based on speculation and or probability. To assert certainly that The Traveller is not alone is a speculative guess – a faith – a religion.

Yet what is quite marvellous and quite revealing is that this is not a question that anyone asks (outside of the philosophical classes). It is an ignored question in most world systems and religions. In fact, I cannot think of a single religion that makes this, one of the most fundamental of questions, a major issue. What is quite fantastic is that there is not a major world religion that declares that The Traveller is God (that you are God) alone in the Universe. Now someone is bound to tell me that I do not understand a particular "ism" and I would reply that if they say that they have not

---

[183] There are many issues here. What would be the nature of our divinity? We can also consider the effects of our decisions with many possible what-if scenarios: for example, what if we are not God and there is an eternal God, what are the consequences of believing that we are God, and vice versa; what if we believe that we are/are not God and there are may gods, etc. This would all be very interesting but not helpful to this discussion. To return to the basic question, the problem is not in doubting that someone is thinking, it is in assuming the nature of "I": perhaps it is more accurate to say "Thinks, therefore Am" rather than "I think, therefore I am."

understood my point. The only evidence that The Traveller can be certain of, is that she is; she and *she alone* is. Why is this not more discussed, why isn't it *the* big question; not "Is there a God?" but "Am I not God?"

If I ask people what is their response to this problem they reply without hesitation "Don't be daft, or course I am not God!" It is as if they have an inner knowledge that tells them so; a knowledge that they trust so completely they are never bothered at all by the question.

We can do a small experiment, firstly on ourselves. My contention is that it is a reasonable assumption, based on the evidence available to assume that you, the only consciousness that you are certain of, are "God." The point at issue is that it is reasonable to assume that you are such a God. But examine yourself carefully, do you really believe that such a possibility is true?

The second experiment that you can do is to ask others if they think that they may be such a God. I doubt that you will find anyone who considers such a possibility likely.

Why is this? Why does such an idea receive such universal rejection? It is as if we *know* that it is untrue. It is as if we have a knowledge that is seemingly in-built. Something inside us tells us to dismiss the possibility.[184]

---

[184] Evolutionists would readily agree with this statement but explain it by saying that we have evolved a genetic response that protects the species from individuals who think that they are God and who therefore believe that they can exercise totalitarian rights. That is good so far as it goes. Such an explanation does not address the issue of how such knowledge came to be. An evolutionist may argue that it evolved through trial and error. We would continue in such debate until we came to a place in which the evolutionist would have to say that what he or she believes in is a working model supported by evidence. To which I would reply, "likewise". The evolutionist has a faith and so do I. I reject completely the idea that one is biased on "science" and not the other. They are both faiths, only one keeps changing.

If this is true, it is remarkable, as it would mean that we do have some knowledge of total-reality and of God from outside of our senses. It would mean that the consciousness that is ours does have at least some contact with total-reality. Moreover, we apparently rely upon this knowledge to form the biggest decisions of our lives, the decisions about who and what we are.

There is, within us all, a still, small voice, which whispers revelation to us.

> *"Then He [the LORD] said, 'Go out, and stand on the mountain before the LORD.' And behold, the LORD passed by, and a great and strong wind tore into the mountains and broke the rocks in pieces before the LORD, but the LORD was not in the wind; and after the wind an earthquake, but the LORD was not in the earthquake; and after the earthquake a fire, but the LORD was not in the fire; and after the fire a still small voice. So it was, when Elijah heard it, that he wrapped his face in his mantle and went out and stood in the entrance of the cave,"* 1 Kings 19:11-13 (NKJ).

In the New Testament Paul talks about such an inner knowledge that is with all of us.

> *"Indeed, when Gentiles, who do not have the law, do by nature things required by the law, they are a law for themselves, even though they do not have the law, since they show that the requirements of the law are written on their hearts, their consciences also bearing witness, and their thoughts now accusing, now even defending them,"* Romans 2:14-15.

What is this nature? It is clearly not taught and it would not seem reasonable to assume that Paul is referring to genetic programming.

What is this nature? It is the still, small voice, the gentle whisper that directs us towards the prompting of God. This is where we discover God and this is where we hear him. He has placed within us all a level of knowledge and the facility to hear him. If we want to grow in him, this is where we will find him.

> "Two things fill the heart with ever renewed and increasing awe and reverence, the more often and the more steadily we meditate upon them: **the starry firmament above and the moral law within.**"[185]

---

[185] Immanuel Kant: *Critique of Pure Reason*, from the concluding section, 1781.

Chapter 5a

The Lost Traveller

- * To find God The Traveller needs to listen
- * Jesus shows the way
- * Sin came into the world through Adam and Eve
- * Three stages of the journey

We can now go on to consider our picture of The Traveller

- * She is existing in a total-reality that is held together and formed by the will of God
- * She has access to part of this total-reality through at she senses we have been calling sense-reality
- * She has a certain amount of on-board genetic data
- * She also has a small inner voice that whispers to her

She rarely ignores her senses. Her genetic information has great significance to her but does not directly influence her decision-making. The inner voice is one she may think that she is ignoring or she may even deny it is there. Nevertheless, it plays a big role in leading her to form the big attitudes of her life, such as who she is. It is a voice from God that she can so easily ignore. Other than that, she is cut off from God: He is not in her sense reality. She is mortal; one day her craft will crash.

She may believe that when her craft ceases so will she and she will cease to exist but it is a contention here that such a thought is not born out by the information around her.[186]

The Traveller is the daughter of Adam and Eve. When they rebelled against God, the effect was to alter the constitution of the whole of total-reality.[187] From their immediate experiential position, they found themselves out of the Garden of Eden and in bodies that had lost the ability to communicate with God in their sense-reality. The Traveller was born into this state and lives within it.

God wants to restore the relationship. The Bible shows us that the future state of those that have restored this relationship is the New Jerusalem and for those that have not it is the lake of fire.

In this life, God places before The Traveller the choice of his Son, Jesus. The Traveller may choose to put her reliance and faith in him or she may not do so.[188] The choice is hers. She gathers information from her sense-reality to help her make this decision. As we have been considering, she can have no significant knowledge of total-

---

[186] See chapter 2: *A Little Religion.*

[187] Romans 8:20-23

[188] To understand the plight of those who have not heard about Jesus, we may consider Romans 2:14-15.

reality and the mind and will of God through her sense-data alone. Her path to God comes through the inner voice.

It is through this voice that God will reach her. It is here that he will convict her of her sin and offer her Jesus. Moreover, it is here that he will judge her. To find God, rather than to think, The Traveller needs to listen.

Let us consider the words of John chapter 3 again:

> *"For God so loved the world that he gave his one and only Son, [Jesus] that whoever believes in him shall not perish but have eternal life. For God did not send his Son into the world to condemn the world, but to save the world through him. Whoever believes in him is not condemned, but whoever does not believe stands condemned already because he has not believed in the name of God's one and only Son. This is the verdict: Light has come into the world, but men loved darkness instead of light because their deeds were evil. Everyone who does evil hates the light, and will not come into the light for fear that his deeds will be exposed. But whoever lives by the truth comes into the light, so that it may be seen plainly that what he has done has been done through God,"* John 3:16-21.

Jesus is pointing out two paths. There are "those who believe in him" who will not perish but *"have eternal life"*, and there are those who do not believe who "stand condemned already because he has not believed in the name of God's one and only Son." Because their deeds are evil, they hate the Light of God and reject him.

The ground on which this choice is made is not our knowledge, not our training, not our tradition or history, not the accident of our birth, our past or our future but our response to the inner voice. To reject that inner voice is the same rejection as Adam and Eves'. In the same way, to reject that voice will be to bring about the same consequence as Adam and Eves' rejection, the penalty of death, and death means removal from the presence of God. When the craft crashes The Traveller's destination will depend upon this choice and this choice alone, the choice she made following the prompting of the inner voice.

Salvation from the effects of sin, the wrath of God and the security of everlasting life within God's favour is only found in the acceptance of Jesus' death and resurrection in the place of our sins.

Paul, in Ephesians chapter 2:1-10, puts it like this:

> *"As for you, you were dead in your transgressions and sins, in which you used to live when you followed the ways of this world and of the ruler of the kingdom of the air, the spirit who is now at work in those who are disobedient. All of us also lived among them at one time, gratifying the cravings of our sinful nature and following its desires and thoughts. Like the rest, we were by nature objects of wrath.*
>
> *"But because of his great love for us, God, who is rich in mercy, made us alive with Christ even when we were dead in transgressions - it is by grace you have been saved. And God raised us up with Christ and seated us with him in the heavenly realms in Christ Jesus, in order that in the coming ages he might show the incomparable riches of his grace, expressed in his kindness to us in Christ Jesus. For it is by grace you have been saved, through faith - and*

this not from yourselves, it is the gift of God – not by works, so that no one can boast. For we are God's workmanship, created in Christ Jesus to do good works, which God prepared in advance for us to do."

Our task is to consider the relationship between The Traveller and the Holy Spirit.

We will look at this as three historical periods:

* The time in The Traveller's life when she was not in fellowship with God
* The time in her life when she accepted God's gift of his Son
* The time in her life when she grew in the Spirit's empowering

This remainder of this chapter will consider the first period, following chapters will consider the other periods.

Let us come back to the picture of The Traveller existing as a craft and a consciousness within it (she may regard herself as the consciousness). The Traveller's consciousness has little or no knowledge of God. She is moving through a total-reality that she is only partly aware of through her senses. Her consciousness has within the craft, somewhere, a facility by which she, the consciousness, can receive information other than through her senses. This information deeply affects her attitude and her belief as to who and what she is. As she journeys on, she may be unconcerned about the conditions of life or the next life or she may be deeply concerned. She is unable to have direct awareness of God and she may or may not be concerned about the questions concerning him that are raised in her experience.

Some time in The Traveller's life she will have an encounter with the Holy Spirit. He will whisper to her through her inner voice. What is important is how she responds.

The Traveller is not in tune with God but in that state of contrariness the Holy Spirit will reach her for a first time. She may or may not remember this event. Once, I asked a Bible study group to recall their experiences of this time. They shared testimonies about their recollections of this first touch. What was common to us all was that we had had an awareness that we had felt through the inner voice that had spoken to us. For many of us it was a comforting presence in a time of difficulty; for others it was a reassurance that they were not alone. This is the ministry of the Holy Spirit. As our lives developed so we began to recognise this voice. Eventually the voice will do two things; it will convict us of our sin and point to Jesus as the answer. There appears to be no set order of doing this and no set time scale. In our group testimonies came from one who said that this process took thirty years and to others in which it took only a few minutes in a meeting. For some this prompting is a gentle whisper. I have met others who had a clear unmistakable revelation of Jesus.

Our response to this inner voice sets us on our journey with God. That there is a voice at all is testimony to God's grace in reaching out to us. He reaches out to us and we must respond. For some, the voice is ignored. If the Holy Spirit's pointing to Jesus goes unanswered, in other words The Traveller ignores it and does not turn to the Light, she commits the sin of Adam and Eve for herself. That would be her condemnation.

If she turns to the Light and follows the Holy Spirit's prompting it will lead her to salvation. The Spirit will open her mind to the things of Christ and she will commit herself to him and accept him as her only grounds of righteousness: her sin taken by his righteousness.

Chapter 6a

Divine Fellowship

* The inner voice
* God created a creature of intelligent free will
* Laws, chance and will
* Retuning to God
* A new creation, new senses

In our narrative The Traveller has come to the place of hearing the inner voice, that place where God speaks to her. In my own story this happened when I was about seventeen. As a youth in the 1960s I had invested some time and energy into exploring areas of life and thought that could be considered as "spiritual." I was developing my views and ideas of life, religion and the like. I was aware of some sort of guidance, a sort of destiny, a feeling that I was on a journey. A journey not to discover "what" but "who". I had had no clear encounter, no moment of decision. This did happen, not in a church or a Christian environment but in a musical folk club. I was with friends on an evening out. I would describe the club as a sort of "bring your own" music event. Talented individuals would take the stage and sing folk ballads, almost always to an acoustic guitar. It was trendy to smoke and for the performer to leave his or her cigarette dangling from the end of the untrimmed guitar string. Aloofness was desirable: we were of the age (as are, have been and will be) of that generation who simultaneously explore environments, inner and outer, whilst at the same time portray an ambience of arrival. To the platform, I was an appreciating listener, not one of the performing elite to whom a sort of guru status had been attributed. A well-known and appreciated young man, a few years older than me, was singing a song, a parody of the American national anthem, possibly some sort of protest about the American war in Vietnam. In all honesty, the message was secondary to the trendy atmosphere of protest and the youthful confidence and superiority to anything that was establishment.

"Be kind to your web footed friends
For that duck may be somebody's muu-ther"

Not the atmosphere in which one may expect an encounter with God. I was certainly not looking for it. But it came, from the inner voice. I heard, saw and felt nothing through my senses but I became aware of a prompting from someone/thing to look around. I did. I may have stood up to do so, I don't recall, but I do recall looking around. What I saw was a sea of smiling and laughing faces (I was sat a few rows off the front; the hall was only about ten or so deep). Then it was as if I saw behind the faces. Each one with its own story, its own hopes and aspirations, its own pain, its own loneliness; the face was a veneer, a cover, it was ephemeral, gone tonight when reality took over. Who was real? The call to me was very clear: choose. Choose between the illusion of the folk club, its signified reality, and the "voice" the prompting. At the time I was not moving in any particular Christian circles, in fact, I was exploring Eastern religions but I knew who was making this challenge; I knew who it was. There was no visible presence, no audible voice but I knew that this was the man from Galilee. Although not audible, it was a still, small voice, it was present, it was real. I chose.

What I had been prepared for was the message from the inner voice, the prompting from the Holy Spirit who showed me Jesus. He will reach us all in a different way. My experience will not be the same as The Traveller's, but there will be similarities. The Traveller, if she wants to come back into relationship with God, will hear a challenge; it may be sudden, it may be over many years, but there will be a call to turn away from values that are not God's and to turn to those that are. There will be a requirement, and a desire, to share with others that this comes from Jesus.

Why is there a need to come back into a relationship with God? How did The Traveller loose it? She lost it as part of the human race when Adam and Eve lost humanity's relationship with God. Let us spend a few moments exploring this accepting that it is not possible for those that God created to fully understand his mind. To allow divisions and schism between those who seek to obey him over areas of doctrine to be defeated, Christ calls us to live in unity. However, we are called to understand what we can notwithstanding the challenge of maintaining fellowship with those who, although clearly in relationship with Christ, see things differently than we do. Having made the warning, please allow me to try to outline the unfathomable process of creation from God's perspective; a task that I am bound to fail in. Nevertheless, it is a task that may richly reward us if you would allow me the impossible approximations and allegories with which I will aim to bring the ineffable into the ordinary.

If we may ignore concepts like the timelessness of God, who created time, and place him in a time reality, purely to aide our understanding, we may come to conceive the following.

Consider that there was once a reality that was God alone. In this reality, there is nothing other than God. God is not lonely or needing fellowship or needing anything, he is self-sufficient and self-supporting. From this timeless eon, due to his character and grace, God resolves the following – he will form a creature with whom he can fellowship:

* This creature will fellowship with him from the position of choice; in other words it will choose to fellowship with God

* If it is to choose it must have the free will to choose to do so, or to choose not to

So, God's self imposed task is to create a creature of intelligent free will.

Murphy's Law is variously described. As I understand it, it is not a law at all but an observation that says that if a thing can go wrong, given long enough, it will. It can also be seen as an application of a statistical reality but it is not confined just to statistics. From a statistical viewpoint, it means that if the bad outcome from an event is a one in a ten chance, if you have about ten goes at the event you have a reasonable chance of getting one bad outcome. If you have a hundred goes at it, you can be fairly certain that the bad outcome will happen. If you keep on doing it all the time you can be totally certain that it will happen at some time.

Not to push the allegory too far but God knows all about Murphy's Law. He knows that if he creates a being with free will, it will, in some way or other at some time, rebel, disown and hate him. If it did not it would never have had true spiritual free will.[189] What I am leading up to is this; from the instant that God resolved to make humanity, he knew that he would have to rescue it.

The question is often asked, "Why did God make the creation that he did?" The only answer is that we do not know, he is God, but it may have something to do with the free will of humanity. God made a creation that could contain a humanity with a free moral and spiritual will.

In order to make this creation God knew he would need a plan for a redemption.

God formed what we have been calling total-reality. The only purpose for total-reality is to support and provide an environment that supports the existence of humanity. (It follows that the things that we cannot sense or know, are there to support what we can and do know.) God's rules for this creation follow the rules of his own nature.[190] We are not in a position to ask why God is like he is, he is what he is.[191] God is unchanging, immutable, and he made his creation on immutable laws.

We have no problem understanding this when we come to observe the creation as we can see it, that is what is apparent to our sense-reality. The laws of physics are fixed. They do not change on a day-

---

[189] I am not suggesting that the fall was a chance event! I am only using Murphy's Law as an illustration that if a thing can go wrong, it will. The fall was a deliberate choice. It was a choice that was made from the position of a will that could make that choice. We could consider the fact of the fall as the demonstration of the evidence that Adam had the free will to make the bad decision. A point could be made to say that if Adam had not fallen his will could never have been truly free. I am suggesting that God knew that if he gave Adam a free choice, Adam would eventually make the wrong one.

[190] The rules that govern God are God's rules.

[191] Exodus 3:14.

to-day basis; the force of gravity is the same everyday, the laws of motion are the same everywhere. We can see that there are fixed and unchanging rules that govern the universe. (We could see science as the quest to understand and reveal those laws.) From these laws other forces work. An animal does not have a predictable life, but its life is based upon these predictable forces: its body works according to set laws; for example, it needs to eat according to its energy requirements. These laws also allow a measure of chance. If I play dice, I can create chance, but only within the framework of set laws. In other words, when we throw the dice it behaves according to the laws of physics, but the result of throwing it creates the opportunity for chance. Within our sense-reality there is both chance and will, but these are framed and held within a context of immutable laws. In summary, God created the universe by setting laws, the effects of which allow chance and will.

God set these laws, he does not change them and he does not ignore them. They do not bind him as he may ignore them. When this happens, we see the miraculous. We can understand a miracle as an event that, by God's sovereign will and action, bypasses the immutable laws of science. It is important to understand that miracles do not hold the universe together; they flow against God's creative stream. There are some laws that God never breaks or changes. We can play word games and create ideas that show this, for example, God cannot decide that there will be no God.[192]

The laws of science show us that God has created the universe, both seen and unseen, according to rules and laws. He can break those laws as sovereign miracles. He does not change his own nature, which is fixed. To debate whether he could or could not change his

---

[192] This is a field that has amused many sophists: is God not omnipotent if he cannot remove himself, or if he cannot lie? Etc., etc., etc..

nature is pure sophistry and unprofitable, he has shown us that he does not.

The purpose of drawing this analogy is to help us understand that God's nature governs the fixed laws of God's reality in the same way that the laws of science govern our reality. We cannot describe God's nature according to mathematical laws. He describes the laws of his nature to us in the teachings and stories of the Bible. We can understand these within the limits of our humanity and conceive God to have proprieties such as grace, love, fairness, and a desire to fellowship, to mention a few. We can even have some understanding that God created us in order to express his nature.

God has an immutable nature. Parts of this nature are the laws of justice and balance. God is forgiving, loving and just. These are not contradictory but part of the balanced, whole and perfect nature of God.

When God created the world that he gave to Adam and Eve he was appreciated by them with their sense-reality. He was in relationship and harmony with them. They chose to break this relationship and harmony. Breaking such a relationship, the purpose of which was the whole reason for creation, offended the very nature of God. The offence caused Adam and Eve to live in a changed sense-reality, a fallen one, one in which they could not live with God whom they had spurned. After this rebellion, Adam and Eve were separated from God and God had lost the very fellowship that he sought to create. God was spurned and angry, Adam and Eve were lost from God's eternal presence. This was the inevitable consequence due to the unchanging nature of God.

Let us go back now and consider that moment in which God decides to create a universe to house humanity. A number of things happen.

* God knows he will create a Universe according to his nature
* He knows that if he creates a humanity with a free will that humanity will rebel and offend that which is his own nature
* He knows that his nature will be offended and will need to see justice
* He knows that if he creates a free willed humanity, he will need to find away for that humanity to return to him after the inevitable fall

What I am saying is that the moment God decided to create humanity with a free will he decided to give a way back to him following the inevitable fall. This is also his nature, a nature of love and forgiveness.

We must consider the effects of this rebellion a little more. To rebel against God is to rebel against all that there is. Adam and Eve did not simply fall out with God, that is, have a little spat that a bit of talking could resolve. They chose to eat of knowledge of good and evil. In other words, they chose to become as God, to replace God. There was no evil in the Garden of Eden; they chose to know good from evil, that is to know evil. Evil is that which is not God; it is anti-God.[193] This is what they chose. They chose a path that would lead to their suffering, to their alienation from God, and ultimately, to their eternity being not with God but with anti-God, that is evil.[194]

---

[193] Like anti-Matter is to Matter.

[194] We may ask why there is evil. Evil is the result of the choice. If evil could not have existed the choice could not have been made and the will would not have been truly free.

The effect of the fall was to visit evil upon the creation and upon humanity. The effect of God's nature was to pour his anger and wrath upon those who choose evil.

If God was to find away back for humanity he needed to allow the expression of his own wrath and to find a resolution (or we may think of it like an antidote) to his wrath.

At the moment of deciding to create humanity God knew that:

* Due to the inevitable rebellion, he would pour his whole wrath and anger out upon those who choose suffering and evil
* To find away back he would have to receive upon himself his whole wrath and anger to shield humanity from it

So God expresses his love and anger. His anger would be poured out on humanity in eternity; his love would take that eternal anger onto himself.

God did this by coming into his creation as a human, living a perfect life yet being killed for that life. In death, God would visit upon himself his own entire wrath.

God planned Calvary at the same instant as he planned creation. There would be no creation without Calvary. Calvary was both the expression of God's love and the resolution of his anger.

The moments in time that we call Calvary are just as much the beginning of all time as is the moment that God spoke the creation into being. God is timeless and exists in all time. All time looks forward to and backwards on Calvary.

When God decided to make humanity with a free will, he hung himself upon the cross to redeem humanity and to propitiate, that is to satisfy, his own wrath. He knew it was the inevitable consequence of his own nature, that of love and justice. There is no pain in this world that he did not endure and no punishment in the next that he has not taken.

Let us come back to The Traveller. The Bible tells us what the rebellion of Adam and Eve needed in order to reunite God with his created beings.

1. The Bible says that The Traveller needs to be justified; the Greek word used is *dikaiosune,* which contains within it the idea of being made acceptable to God.

> *"This righteousness from God comes through faith in Jesus Christ to all who believe. There is no difference, for all have sinned and fall short of the glory of God, and are justified freely by his grace through the redemption that came by Christ Jesus. God presented him as a sacrifice of atonement, through faith in his blood. He did this to demonstrate his justice, because in his forbearance he had left the sins committed beforehand unpunished – he did it to demonstrate his justice at the present time, so as to be just and the one who justifies those who have faith in Jesus,"* Romans 3:22-26.

2. The Bible says that God needs to be propitiated; the Greek word used is *hilasmos,* which contains within it the idea of appeasement.

> *"And he is the propitiation for our sins: and not for ours only, but also for the sins of the whole world,"* 1 John 2:2 (KJV).

When The Traveller hears and obeys the call from the Holy Spirit's prompting these two problems are removed through the ministry of Jesus' death and resurrection. How and what happens is, to my mind, unknowable. It is clear that the event of Jesus' life, death and resurrection had effects not just on humanity but upon God as well. We are unable to comprehend it. We do not have the necessary senses to appreciate God's reality.

We are aware of the results.

There is a two-fold result. Firstly we have the promise, the certainty, of being raised in a new body (1 Corinthians 15:43-44). Just as the death of Adam and Eve lead to the corruption of the body, so The Traveller's physical death will now lead to a new body; one that will live in both time and space, a new time and space.[195] Secondly, there is the reality of a new living relationship with God that starts in this sense-reality, in this time.

The promise of a new body is such a certainty to Paul that he mocks the fear of death.

> *"Listen, I tell you a mystery: We will not all sleep, but we will all be changed – in a flash, in the twinkling of an eye, at the last trumpet. For the trumpet will sound, the dead will be raised imperishable, and we will be changed. For the perishable must clothe itself with the imperishable, and the mortal with immortality. When the perishable has been clothed with the imperishable, and the mortal with immortality, then the saying that is written will come true: 'Death has been*

[195] Revelation 21 and 22 clearly show both time and space.

wallowed up in victory.' 'Where, O death, is your victory? Where, O death, is your sting?'

The sting of death is sin, and the power of sin is the law. But thanks be to God! He gives us the victory through our Lord Jesus Christ. Therefore, my dear brothers, stand firm. Let nothing move you. Always give yourselves fully to the work of the Lord, because you know that your labour in the Lord is not in vain," 1 Corinthians 15:51-58.

So is the future state, what about the present?

The new relationship starts for The Traveller the moment that she accepts Christ.

The new body will bring the full restoration but until then The Traveller continues in her Adamic body subject to its failings, ills and tendencies. But this is the old body with added value! So much added value that Paul is inclined to refer to it as new.

"Therefore, if anyone is in Christ, he is a new creation; the old has gone, the new has come! All this is from God, who reconciled us to himself through Christ and gave us the ministry of reconciliation: that God was reconciling the world to himself in Christ, not counting men's sins against them. And he has committed to us the message of reconciliation," 2 Corinthians 5:17-19.[196]

---

[196] Paul may be referring to the eternal body as well. The work of redemption is one work, what The Traveller has after her decision to follow Jesus now is part of what she already has to come; she already has it, just not yet got it.

So what is new?

We have observed that The Traveller, in her not-reconciled-to-God state was able to hear and have some contact with God, I am referring to the still small voice. Whether this voice belongs to The Traveller or is a messenger from God is not, at least to me, very clear. It is a way that the Holy Spirit may contact her. Whatever its origins and status it is a contact between The Traveller and God.[197] As such it indicates that part of The Traveller has some contact with the reality outside of herself.

After her reconciliation to God there is a real change. Now there is a permanent two-way communication system set up that is The Traveller's, or to phrase that a little more accurately, is The Traveller. The Traveller may need to become accustomed to this, to learn of its power and limitations but she will find that in various ways the voice of God becomes clearer to her and that she can, through prayer, commune with God. This may take some learning. She will realise that by using this facility she will be able to make changes in the reality that is outside of her senses; in other words, God answers prayer.[198]

If we recall The Traveller's nature we will see that she is a being that is held in existence by the nature of God, as is all creation. She is aware, through her senses, of a reality that we have called her sense-reality. There are things that exist outside of her sense-reality but she is not equipped to sense them. Some of The Traveller's own being must exist outside of her own sense reality or she would by unable to hear the inner voice. In her new, reconciled-to-God state it is in these areas that the biggest changes occur. She will learn that prayer is the tool by which she can affect the reality that she may

---

[197] We must be careful to distinguish between God and total-reality.

[198] He answers prayer, he does not take orders.

not see, but she may see the effects within her reality. For the Jews at the time of Christ on earth the Jewish Temple was the facility by which the devout could find and hear from God. Now, in this new divine fellowship, the reconciled Traveller can consult and enjoy God through the facility that she can find within herself.

Chapter 7a

Assurance

* Individuality, commonality
* Trust

Like all new relationships, The Traveller's relationship with God will be individual to her. It would be quite a mistake to suggest that it will develop in a specific way as if it were on a sort of program, it will not. It will grow and change in a way that is unique to her.

But like all relationships there will be aspects of it that are common to others. These aspects of her relationship may all be happening at the same time and taking on different levels of significance to her at different times of her life. She will be very aware that she has moved from a relationship in which she wondered about God into one in which she wonders with God.

Her journey will have been one in which she, in retrospect, may recognise stages. She will have been through a period in her life in which she had little interest in God, then a period in which God had been challenging her. This would have led to the time when she will have responded to God. All these stages will have been mediated through the Holy Spirit. Now she will enter the rest of her life, a life in which she can grow and develop her relationship with God in the way that is individual to her.

It would be quite unwise to suggest that this relationship can be neatly packaged up into simple hurdles to jump or into merits to acquire but it is helpful to consider that her growth will be in different fields that can be identified. There are a number of these, all with very indistinct boundaries. Simple, straightforward knowledge of God and the Bible is one, character development another; prayer, trust and faith would be others.

At this point in our story The Traveller has come to a place in her life where she has:

* Recognised that God is speaking to her
* Through the prompting of the Holy Spirit, she has recognised God's pointing to Jesus
* She has learnt that God requires three things of her: To decide to turn away from following her ways and to turn towards following his; to recognise that Jesus, being God in the flesh, has paid the price for her sin and propitiated God; to confess that he has done this for her, he alone. She will know that she cannot do this for herself, neither in part nor in whole

Once she has found that, in her heart, these things have happened, she will begin to notice changes in her life and within herself. These changes occur in different people at different times and in different ways. One of the first changes she will note is an assurance of her forgiveness and her acceptance by God.

> *"For God so loved the world that he gave his one and only Son, that whoever believes in him shall not perish but have eternal life,"* John 3:16.

She will start to feel confident that this applies to her. This confidence does not always come easily or immediately.

> *"that whoever* ***believes,*** *in him shall not perish but have eternal life."*

The Greek word that is translated "believe" (*pisteuo*) has a wider meaning than "to accept as fact". It leans more towards the concept of "trust in".[199]

I trust that my computer works. I do not understand how. Sometimes I sincerely doubt that it will work but, nevertheless, I place my thoughts and documents into its care.

Jesus did not say, "that whoever understands / agrees with / gives mental assent shall not perish but have eternal life" but something more like, "that whoever **trusts,** in me shall not perish but have eternal life."

Trust, in this context, is shown by what we do rather than by what we think.

We are not asked to accept without questioning or to fully understand, we are asked to trust. Trust is built by intelligent questioning. It develops by understanding God's teaching.[200]

If I trust a bridge, I will stand on it. I may not like it or understand it, I may even doubt it. Nevertheless, when the time of crossing comes, what matters is whether I stand on it. By standing on it, I show my trust despite my doubt.

---

[199] John 14.1 for example where *pisteuo* is translated as "trust in".

[200] Romans 10:17.

The Traveller finds that despite her doubts, questions, fears and difficulties, despite the fact that on one day she feels one way and on another day she may feel another, what matters is, that she trusts in Jesus.

The Traveller's actions show this trust, which is an internal conviction.

For some people this trust just happens. It seems to be born inside of them by the Holy Spirit despite their intellectual objections. They come to a place in which they observe that deep down inwardly they do trust Jesus although their minds may not be so sure.

Others have no questions or doubts at all, they just trust.

Others still need to make a commitment to trust. This can come in the form of a pledge to God or a confession of faith, a little like the three Hebrew witnesses Shadrach, Meshach and Abednego in Daniel 3.They told the King that no matter what he did they would trust in their God; no matter what, they would trust.

Job said; *"Though he slay me, yet will I hope in him,"* Job 13:15.

Peter said; *"Lord, to whom shall we go? You have the words of eternal life. We believe and know that you are the Holy One of God,"* John 6:68-69.

What matters is not the extent of our doubt but the extent of our trust. Do we trust our eternal lives to him? We can test this, not by what our minds challenge us with but by what gives our internal souls peace. The Traveller's mind may struggle but she will find deep internal peace when she places her trust in Jesus. He said, *"Do not let your hearts be troubled. Trust in God; trust also in me,"* John 14:1.[201]

---

[201] The Greek word for trust here is *pisteuo*, the same word that is translated as "believe" in John 3:16.

The Traveller will find that this trust will work its way out into her life. She will hear the Holy Spirit in her conscience much more readily. She will start to seek out and enjoy the company and fellowship of other Christians and she will want to and be blessed by obedience to the Christian disciplines such as giving, water baptism, and worship.

She will start to pray. She will start to worship. She will seek to find ways of serving God, to minister. She will know that she has become a child of God.

> *"We know that we have come to know him if we obey his commands. The man who says, 'I know him,' but does not do what he commands is a liar, and the truth is not in him. But if anyone obeys his word, God's love is truly made complete in him. This is how we know we are in him: Whoever claims to live in him must walk as Jesus did," 1 John 2:3-6.*

Chapter 8a

The Old and The New

* Spiritual growth
* Flesh and Spirit
* Examine yourself

All adults were once children. All adults have been through the various stages of childhood. It is possible to describe and define stages in child development but it is not possible to say that every child will develop in the same way. In other words, all adults were once teenagers but that does not mean to say that all adults had the same teenage experience: all adults were once two years old but that does not mean to say that all adults were once "terrible"![202]

Developmental stages exist but each individual goes through them individually. Some may have found teenage years easy, others may not have; some may have been delightful winsome toddlers, others

[202] There is an urban folk-lore that describes the toddler as being at the age of the "terrible two's".

demanding and whining. If we define the stages of growth, we are not defining the individual.

It is the same with spiritual growth. We can recognise stages and in hindsight, we can see how we, as individuals, went through those stages, but we will all make a uniquely individual passage. This story of The Traveller is looking at the stages in a broad sense. It is not saying how each individual will make the passage. This is true for each of the stages of her spiritual life.

The first stage is from rebellion to conviction. We have looked at how The Traveller is made up and how the Holy Spirit offers her guidance to Jesus. Then we have considered how she first hears the Holy Spirit and how she starts to listen. This is the stage from conviction to conversion. As she listens she will come to the same place that Thomas found when he said to Jesus *"My Lord and my God."*[203] She will repent of her old ways and place her faith in Christ's death and resurrection. She will own a salvation that is born from her faith in him and not from any sense of her own self worth. She will find an assurance of her heavenly destiny. She will start to pray. She will start to worship. She will seek to obey God's commands in areas such as baptism. She will start to read and understand God's word in the Bible. She will fellowship with other Christians. All these things (and others) will start to happen in her life but they will not start in the same order or with the same intensity in each individual. What is happening is that she is developing a relationship with God not obeying a system of credits.

As she starts to do and seek these things, she has entered into the stage of equipping. God will equip her to serve and grow in her new relationship with him. There are many parts of this relationship. We

---

[203] John 20:28

are going to consider three areas that are common to all who grow in Christ. These three areas are:

* The relationship between The Traveller's old self and her new self
* The use and submission of her natural abilities
* The giving and use of new spiritual abilities

We will consider them as three distinct areas as that makes our task of understanding easier. We will keep in mind that they are three areas that overlap, exist together, do not come or change in any particular order and that we all experience these things differently and individually.

The Traveller is complex. We have considered some aspects of her. She has skills and attitudes that she has developed and others that she was born with: her environment will affect her as will her genetic make up. When she becomes a Christian, she finds that she has a relationship with God in which the Holy Spirit directs her and points her to Jesus. Paul says that, *"Therefore, if anyone is in (en) Christ, he is a new creation; the old has gone, the new has come!"* 2 Corinthians 5:17.

He also says, when talking to Christians, *"Brothers, I could not address you as spiritual but as worldly – mere infants in Christ,"* 1Corinthians 3:1.

The picture that builds up is that The Traveller is becoming a new person. This does not happen all at once. She will become aware of two pressures in her life. One will be the tendency to rebel against the Spirit's leading and the other will be a desire to follow the Spirit's leading.

Paul links these two tendencies to The Traveller's two loyalties, the past loyalty of her old ways, that is the ways of her physical make up and the new loyalty to the leading of the Spirit.[204] We will call these "the inborn way" and "spiritual way".

It is a mistake to see The Traveller as either one or the other, she is not either the old inborn self or the new spiritual self; she is a mixture of both. In some areas, she may be mainly spiritual and in other things she may owe more of herself to the old inborn tendencies. She may be able to think of individuals who have shown remarkable competencies in areas of ministry only to find out that they have had deep hidden sin in their life. If she is growing spiritually, she will consider her own failings. The Traveller is a mixture of both factors. God's desire is for her to grow in stature as a spiritual being and to shrink the bulk that makes up her old inborn nature.

The Traveller's old inborn way will lead her to follow attitudes and actions that come from her inner fears and desires for self-preservation. She may have decided to trust Jesus but her old nature will take some time to get used to this. She enters into a life long struggle against the inborn way. God will tell her to do to others as she would have done to herself. She will try and live like this but the old inborn way will tell her to grab first and ask questions later. She will want to find more time to worship and serve God but the old inborn way will soon start to point out that time spent in front of the TV is relaxing and, it will claim, time well spent: wouldn't it just. She must not overwork, the inborn way will say, better take an evening off and watch the box.

She will start to notice that the battlefield will be her attitudes and her actions. The way that she does things will be as important as what she does.

---

[204] Paul calls one the *sarkinois* which literally means "fleshy" and the other *pneumatikos* which literally means "of the spirit". 1 Cor.3:1-3.

As she grows and develops as a Christian, she will face the problem of wrestling with the inborn self. There may come a time when she is prepared to stop growing. She may decide, consciously or other wise, to continue in many of her old ways. This often becomes apparent in her choice of friends and entertainment. She may not do things that are offensive to God but she may cease to seek only those things that are pleasing to God. Her prayer life may change. She may stop seeking God's will for areas of her life that she wants to control. She may not give those areas in trust to him.

She can always examine herself to see how much of herself is the new spiritual person and how much is the old inborn person. She can ask herself questions about her attitudes:

* Does she feel comfortable when praised and given glory?
* Does she get upset when her pride is hurt?
* Does she feel hurt when her service for God is not noticed or praised?
* Is she jealous of those who show more ability than her?
* Does she harbour resentment to those who lead?
* Does she work harder for God and pray more fervently when she is noticed and praised?
* Does she welcome Godly discipline and correction?
* Does she keep a certain distance from the centre of spiritual work?
* Are her prayers directed towards God fulfilling her desires rather than she fulfilling God's?

It is a salutary lesson to think of more questions that she may ask. When we ask ourselves such questions we will find that every one of us, if we are honest, will have to admit to some degree of weakness in many of these areas. What The Traveller, and we, will benefit from is examining ourselves and gaining a picture of how spiritually motivated we are and how much we are motivated by our old inborn self.

As The Traveller grows in her relationship with God, she will find three principles that impact upon her life:

* The principle of blessing
* The principle of discipline
* The principle of joy and the fruit of the Spirit [205]

She will become much more aware of the Spirit's working in her life. Her first experience of the Spirit would have been the Spirit prompting and guiding her towards repentance and seeking Jesus. Then she will have experienced the Spirit's guiding her through to the place where she can call Jesus her Lord and her God. As she grows, the Spirit will be guiding her towards growing as a spiritual person and dying to the old inborn nature. As she learns to live as God would have her to live, she will note that God's blessing comes into her life. This is not to say that she will not know challenge, sorrow and suffering – a look at the martyrdom of the apostles will show her that. It does not mean that she will become wealthy, or that she should seek to become wealthy – Paul was not and did not. It does mean that within her relationship with God she will notice experiences, endowments, protection, encouragements, confidences, joy, peace and many other gifts that she will identify as being blessings from God.

She will note that God is slow to judge and slow to condemn but through his love, he will discipline her when she ceases to live as God would have her. This discipline can be difficult and painful. God disciplines those he loves:

> *"For the Lord disciplines him whom he loves, and chastises every son whom he receives. It is for discipline that you have to endure. God is treating you as sons; for what son is there whom his father does not discipline? If you are left without discipline, in which all have participated, then you are illegitimate children and not sons. Besides this, we have had earthly fathers to discipline us and we respected them. Shall we not much more be subject to the Father of spirits and live? For they disciplined us for a short time at their pleasure, but he disciplines us for our good, that we may share his holiness. For the moment all discipline seems painful rather than pleasant; later it yields the peaceful fruit of righteousness to those who have been trained by it,"* Hebrews 12:6-11 RSV.

She will note that God's blessing and discipline will lead to her life becoming more Christ like. Her reward, in this life, will be God's joy, which can transcend all else.

> *"But we work with you for your joy, because it is by faith you stand firm,"* 2 Corinthians 1:24.

The Traveller's personality is something that emanates from her craft; from her DNA. It may be moulded by qualities such as her upbringing family and parents, environment, early friendships and education. Her character emanates from the interface of her personality and her consciousness. This, to, will be moulded by her opportunities and challenges. If her personality changes little, her character can develop and change through out her life. As she allows the Holy Spirit to engage her, becoming submissive to the Spirit's leading, she will notice that it is from within her character that fruit will show. She will bear the fruit, but the Spirit will instigate and sustain it; it is the Spirit's fruit, she is the branch. This will not be a sudden change, as it will be born from discipleship and effort. The qualities of love, joy, patience, kindness, goodness, faithfulness, gentleness and self-control will be seen in her character whatever her personality.

> *"But the fruit of the Spirit is love, joy, peace patience, kindness, goodness, faithfulness, gentleness and self-control. Against such things there is no law. Those who belong to Christ Jesus have crucified the sinful nature with its passions and desires. Since we live by the Spirit, let us keep in step with the Spirit. Let us not become conceited, provoking and envying each other,"*
>
> Galatians 5:22-23.

Chapter 9a

I Can Climb A Wall!

"With your help I can advance against a troop; with my God I can scale a wall."
Psalm 18:29

* Gifts and skills
* Learning to surrender, learning partnership

The Traveller, as we have seen, is a complex creature. We are trying to simplify all aspects of her to help us understand her relationship with God. We have considered what happens to the part of her that consists of her character and personality, the home of her emotions and attitudes. She is challenged to change from being led by her old inborn nature towards becoming the person that the Holy Spirit would have her to be, that is, to be spiritual. Now we will look at that part of her that we would define by her abilities and skills. God wants those as well.

The Traveller will be good at some things, better at others and not so good at some, like us all. What God will turn her into is yet to be seen but now she is who and what she is. She will have a wealth of natural abilities and a whole lot of weaknesses. As she grows in the Spirit, becoming more spiritual and owing less to her old ways, she will find the Spirit working on her natural abilities and talents. Let me stress again we are looking at a relationship between The Traveller and God, mediated through the Holy Spirit. Our story about The Traveller is helping us to see the principles, not create rules. What I am not saying is that as she grows in the Spirit her abilities and talents will change in a predictable way; they will change but in a way that Sovereign God decides. There is no fixed formula between spiritual growth and her natural abilities but there is a relationship.

With the Spirit's help, The Traveller will start to become more aware of her strengths and weakness, particularly, as with the Spirit's encouragement she will be able to become more honest with herself. As she grows in God, as she becomes more in tune with the Spirit's values, her old feelings of insecurity and self-doubt will be changed into the security that comes from peace with God. Her progress in this growth will be related to her effort. If she seeks to remove the old sinful ways and turns away from them, sometimes with tears of confession and regret for her own sin, sometimes with the joy of loosing a burden, she will become more in tune with the Spirit. If she tarries in the old ways, making excuses for her sin and weaknesses she will grow more slowly.

She will see herself more clearly becoming more self-aware. She will discover that some natural abilities that she did not previously value are highly valued by God. Conversely, she will find that God detests some of her other most proudly held abilities.

She may have had a talent for shoplifting. Now, as a Christian, both she and God do not value this particular ability. She may have a talent for being seen as a warm and trusted personality. Both God and she will value this talent (unless she uses it to deceive and go shoplifting). She may have known that she was a good singer but never valued the ability and never used her voice. Now, in the context of a church choir or singing group, she may value that ability highly. She may never have known that she was a good listener, preferring to dominate discussion, but now, through the Spirit she may discover this talent. She may then discover that this previously unused ability is the one that God most highly commends.

Different abilities will mean different things to different people. There is no league table of desirable abilities. There is only the value of submitting them to God. Once The Traveller starts to do this, she may start to see her abilities in a different light. She is, after all, only what God made. She may be responsible for her sin (and she has submitted that back to God) but she may begin to see that all her abilities and talents are only contained in the person that she is. Moreover, God made her so and gave her these abilities. She will come to the place where she will see her natural abilities as God given gifts. As gifts, she will be able to give them back to him.

She will find immense confidence in discovering this. God has given unique natural gifts to her. He intends her to use and enjoy them. As she gives them to him, she will discover another principle. The more she gives, the more he empowers.

There was once a woodsman. His job was to go into the wood and fell trees. He became a Christian and God told him to continue to be a woodsman. He did. Every day he went into the wood and cut down trees. One day he realised that this was what God wanted him to do; it was his ministry and calling. He prayed to God saying that if this was what God wanted him to do he would gladly do it. He gave his wood cutting ability to God. Very soon, he began to notice something. He did not get so tired, his axe stayed sharper and the trees did not seem to be so hard. They began to fall down in the easy places. He realised that God was with him and helping him. He gave his thanks to God.

God said to him that he should continue to be a woodsman but he should grow closer to himself and learn to trust in him more. The woodsman did not quite understand how or what he should do to fulfil this so he just prayed and talked to God as he cut down trees and sought to please God in his life. One day as he was chopping away, he heard an almighty crash and a tree fell down beside him. As he chopped it up so did another. The more he chopped the more trees seemed to fall around him.

"What's going on God?" he asked.
"I'm helping," said God.

And so it was, as the woodsman chopped God worked along side him, and when the woodsman rested so did God.

As the woodsman aged and got older he learned that if he walked close to God and trusted then God would work along side him but when he strayed from his fellowship with God then God seemed to help him less. A time came when the woodsman stopped chopping one day and said that he was tired and needed more rest. So he sat down and gave the time in fellowship and worship to God. But this time when he stopped God did not, God carried on chopping.

"What's going on God?" said the woodsman.
"When you are weak, then you are strong," said God.

The woodsman learnt that all he needed to do was to rise up in the morning, sharpen his axe, go to the woods, and start his work with worship. Down fell the trees.

There are stories in the Bible that illustrate this point, that if we give our natural gifts to God, he will augment them, work with us in them, and even work miraculously through them. I like the one-liner in Psalm 18. When we read the psalms we can easily forget that the experiences that David had were not allegorical, they were real. When he said, *"They have tracked me down, they now surround me, with eyes alert, to throw me to the ground."* he meant it.[206] He was tracked down, he was surrounded, and there was an army that was trying to kill him. When he said, *"With your help I can advance against a troop; with my God I can scale a wall,"* he meant it.[207] David was using his own strength. But he was using his own strength multiplied and blessed by God. David knew that place where his own natural gifts could become miraculous in God's providence. Clearly, this did not happen all the time but David knew that in times of crisis, with God with him, he could, literally, climb an un-climbable wall.[208]

The Traveller will find this. She will learn that her natural abilities are God given gifts. She will find that as she surrenders these to him, he will use them. As she grows in God so her gifts will be blessed and she will find that she will be much more effective in what she does as God works with her. If she walks away from his ways, she will notice that she may loose that blessing. She will keep

---

[206] Psalm 17:11

[207] Psalm 18: 29

[208] Neither this story nor the story of the woodsman are meant to imply that all we have to do is sit down and worship and let God do the rest. The woodsman was brought to that place after years of obedient discipleship in which he learnt when to wait and when to act. David's life was one of faith and activity with discipline and blessing. We could easily imagine the story of the less-spiritual woodsman who went into the forest, sat on a log and said to God, "Go on, chop!" He is still giving orders and claiming to see, with something he calls "faith" but I would call wishful thinking, stack loads of chopped up wood, which I can never see.

the gifts; they are hers. She will find that gifts used in partnership with God are richly blessed – of course.

Chapter 10a

Spiritual Gifts

* The battle between the old, inborn way and the new, spiritual nature
* The submission of natural abilities and talents
* The receiving and use of new spiritual gifts

It will be helpful to consider who and what The Traveller is again. We are seeing her as journeying through the total-reality that surrounds her in the vehicle of her body, her craft. This craft is equipped with certain ways of giving her knowledge about what surrounds her, her senses. This knowledge is incomplete; her senses only sense what they are equipped to sense. There is much that they do not sense. The Traveller draws information about what is around her from these incomplete senses. It may be helpful if we consider The Traveller to be a person in a craft (both craft and the person of the consciousness constituting the entity of The Traveller). The craft is the body, the person is the consciousness. The consciousness is blind to everything outside of the craft except that information that comes into the craft through the three ways that the craft, and thus the person of the consciousness, can assimilate. The three ways being: that of natural senses, genetic programming and the small voice that whispers the revelation of God.

This consciousness relies on these ways to understand her place in total-reality. She started to listen to the inner voice that she discovered to be the Holy Spirit. She will have had other inner voices which are not from the Spirit but she has learnt to recognise who the Spirit is and is getting more proficient at hearing and following. [209] By following the Spirit's leading she has journeyed from a place of alienation from God to recognition of God's provision for her. She found this in Jesus, in his death and resurrection. She is beginning to understand her own sin and its consequences. She has come to a place where her desire is to be useful to God. She has moved from a place of rebellion to a place in which she desires to be a servant. Jesus describes this as being reborn.[210]

Amongst the many blessings and lessons of her spiritual growth she will have found two things that happen to her:

---

[209] The Spirit will be recognisable by his qualities and work. He will always glorify Jesus and point to him; he will minister in the direction of convicting the world of sin, righteousness and judgement; his manner will be as his fruit. False spirits will magnify mankind or specific leaders; tend to offer what the hearers want (often promising it miraculously); and not always show the Spirit's character. Recently I listened to a preacher who claimed to be Spirit led spend ten minutes telling the congregation what he was going to do for them, which was to miraculously answer their desires, spend a further thirty minutes telling them what he had done elsewhere, and then explain that this was all done from the strength of his faith. Scripture warns us that such "super apostles" will come. Consider 2 Corinthians 11:20.

[210] John 3:16.

* there are spiritual changes in her life that she will have discovered just seem to happen within her
* and there are spiritual changes and blessings that she has to seek

She will probably notice that some things are more seeking and others more waiting; some things she has to actively seek and others require her passive submission. Most things contain an element of both. The Holy Spirit will never overpower her. In the scripture, every time the Spirit overpowered an individual it was in judgement. The Spirit will always work within the confines of her will. Sometimes, when seeking a blessing or a gift, she may sit, passively, waiting for God to act upon her. When he does not it is because he will be waiting for her to show faith by reaching out.

When she made the step from being distanced from God to being close to God, she will have noticed that the step contained both the elements of waiting and reaching. She had to confess her sin. She had to ask for forgiveness. She had to place her trust in Jesus as being able and willing to provide for her spiritual needs. She had to trust that Jesus is acceptable to God as her mediator. She found within herself a prompting to do this. She found a guiding hand. She found a peace that came into her life and a joy that just seemed to continually bubble away. There were active things that she had to do and passive things that were done within her.

As she grows in God now she will see the same two principles apply; there is her effort and desire and God's quiet working upon and within her. Peter, in his second epistle reminds us of the efforts we must make:

> *"For this very reason, you must make every effort to support your faith with goodness, and goodness with*

> *knowledge, and knowledge with self-control, and self-control with endurance, and endurance with godliness, and godliness with mutual affection, and mutual affection with love. For if these things are yours and are increasing among you, they keep you from being ineffective and unfruitful in the knowledge of our Lord Jesus Christ. For anyone who lacks these things is short-sighted and blind, and is forgetful of the cleansing of past sins. Therefore, brothers and sisters, be all the more eager to confirm your call and election, for if you do this, you will never stumble,"* 2 Peter 1:5-10 NRSV.

Of the world of total-reality much or most, we cannot tell, is hidden from The Traveller. She cannot know it. Her senses are not equipped to report it. Part of this unknown world is God's kingdom. He wants The Traveller to know more of it. In order for her to have access to it, God gives her special senses. These do not operate with the accuracy of her natural senses, at least not at first. As she gets more skilled with them, she may start to rely on them as much. She may receive special senses that allow her to know more of God and his kingdom, allowing her to "see" things that others, who do not have these senses, cannot. She may receive abilities to express God's messages and heart. God can give her any sense or ability that he wants her to have. It is the Holy Spirit who gives all these extra spiritual gifts.[211]

The Traveller may receive them in different ways. Some may be received in a dramatic memorable way. Others, she may slowly discover in herself. Some she may desire and seek, having to take steps of faith in order to receive them. Others may develop quietly

---

[211] See chapter 11.

without her effort to receive them, or to take hold of them. Some may be gifts that are clear to others and have the aura of the supernatural. Others may be a supernatural enhancing of existing abilities. One of the most common is for The Traveller to start to hear the Spirit's voice speaking to her through her Bible reading. She may be used to seeing and discovering God's way through the scripture but she may begin to notice that she enjoys clear prompting from the Spirit over, say, a particular verse. She may have heard others say, "It was as if the verse lit up!" and she may have begun to find the same experience happening in her own reading times. As she walks with God this empowering with such gifts will continue in various ways for the rest of her life.

She may consider that some of these gifts were given to her at the time of her salvation, others may have come and continue to come afterwards. The Holy Spirit is sovereign and has become The Traveller's mentor and teacher, a role the Spirit will always keep.

All these spiritual gifts will have the same purpose. They will build her up in her faith and walk with God and they will build up others. She will start to experience why, in order to function fully as a Christian endowed with God's gifts, she needs to be part of a Spirit led fellowship. She will wish to exercise her gifts and she will wish to benefit from the gifts of others. She will have already found that her well-being is dependent upon her fellowship with God. She will start to see that it is also dependent on her fellowship with others. She will need the benefit of the gifts of others and they will need hers. If she tries to develop spiritually alone, she will be incomplete. She will find that God has designed his Kingdom in such a way as to make all those who are seeking to live in Spiritual harmony dependent upon each other.

All these spiritual gifts will have the same purpose and the same direction. They will always be revealing Jesus.

The Traveller brings to the body of Christ the gift of herself. She is now a very different person from the one who first felt the prompting of the Holy Spirit when she was alienated from God. She brings herself. She brings her natural gifts and abilities. These, she realises are Gods gifts to her as much as any other. She also brings her added gifts, spiritualities that God could only give her after her acceptance into his Kingdom. She comes as a whole person, struggling with the tendencies of her old life and ways and the joys of finding God's ways. All these things serve to give her a role in the church; a unique role that only she can fulfil. She will begin to recognise places and tasks that she fits into and contributions that she can make. We may call this her "gifting". She will come to know this very well, in time. She will learn where her gifting is appropriate and helpful and where it is not. This will be her unique contribution to the church. She will find others with similar gifting and both learn from them and encourage them.

She comes experiencing and enjoying vertical fellowship, fellowship with God, and horizontal fellowship, fellowship with other Christians. She will by no means be perfect, having many faults and weaknesses. She is journeying and she will continue to journey. As she looks back, she will see the journey that she has travelled so far. Through the ministry of the Spirit she will recognise a time past when she did not know God and was a stranger to his kingdom. Now she will be experiencing God's prompting and leading and will see herself as part of God's kingdom, seeking and desiring to work for him.

The Spirit has taken her from one place to another:

> *"What is more, I consider everything a loss compared to the surpassing greatness of knowing Christ Jesus my Lord, for whose sake I have lost all things. I consider them rubbish, that I may gain*

Christ and be found in him, not having a righteousness of my own that comes from the law, but that which is through faith in Christ – the righteousness that comes from God and is by faith.

I want to know Christ and the power of his resurrection and the fellowship of sharing in his sufferings, becoming like him in his death, and so, somehow, to attain to the resurrection from the dead. Not that I have already obtained all this, or have already been made perfect, but I press on to take hold of that for which Christ Jesus took hold of me. Brothers, I do not consider myself yet to have taken hold of it. But one thing I do: Forgetting what is behind and straining toward what is ahead, I press on toward the goal to win the prize for which God has called me heavenward in Christ Jesus. All of us who are mature should take such a view of things. And if on some point you think differently, that too God will make clear to you,"

Philippians 3:8-15.

New Creation

* What we are?
* How we may change?

God created all things. This is one way that we may define God; he is the creator. There is nothing that exists apart from God that he did not create. God maintains all things. There is nothing that can exist separately from God. In other words, there is nothing that can exist on its own apart from God. All things need God to maintain them in order to continue to exist. God exists separately from all time and all space, which he created.

God has a purpose in creating and maintaining time and space. This is so that he may have and enjoy fellowship with us, with humanity. It follows that the purpose of humanity is to enjoy and have fellowship with God. God is separate from his creation but he cares and is involved with it. So much so that he became part of it by becoming human: Jesus was fully man and fully God.

The Traveller exists in the creation that God has made; she is part of that creation. God has equipped her with certain senses and knowledge by which she can know of and interact with other aspects of the creation. She has no way of knowing all of the creation and she does not know what proportion of the creation she does know. God sees and maintains all of his creation. All of creation is total-reality. The Traveller can only know that part of creation that her senses and knowledge will allow. This is her sense-reality.

The Traveller is one being, but like a coin, there are two sides to her; each side depends upon the other for its existence. She has a body and a consciousness, that is, her spacecraft and herself-in-the-spacecraft. When she dies (that is when her spacecraft crashes) her spacecraft will be resurrected into a reality with a new sense-reality. Some believe that this state is the original total-reality; others believe that it is a new one that God has created. To The Traveller it will be a new sense-reality as her new senses will be in tune with those aspects of her resurrection state that God intends. Her place in this resurrection will depend on her relationship with God in her first body, her first sense-reality.

In her first body, her sense-reality is set by the limit of her senses and her inner knowledge. The purpose of her life is to be in fellowship with God. This fellowship has been lost to her due to the exercise of free will, which has and had chosen rebellion to God rather than fellowship. Whilst she is in this state God has reached out to her offering her a way back to him through the life, death and resurrection of Jesus, who is God himself dwelling in a spacecraft, a body. If she accepts God's fellowship God makes some structural changes to her.

These changes take place in her first life, that is, before her resurrection into her second life (her second sense-reality). The first change is that God connects with The Traveller. God, as the Holy Spirit, takes up a place that allows him access to The Traveller's consciousness. The Traveller becomes much more aware of God with whom she can now enter into a relationship. This accommodation of the Holy Spirit is a structural change for The Traveller; it is The Traveller.

The second change is an ongoing consequence of the first. The Holy Spirit, in tandem with The Traveller, begins to offer her gifts. These gifts have a variety of uses, purposes and functions. The Holy Spirit cares for each individual individually. The gifts operate like additional senses. Some gifts may give The Traveller extra information about the world of total-reality around her. Other gifts may give her additional knowledge about God and his mind and will.

In order to have a method of understanding how the gifts work we need a picture of ourselves. The Traveller gives a picture of how the gifts of the Spirit function.

The Traveller represents us all. We are all a consciousness that exists in a physical body. The relationship between our bodies and our consciousness is a very close one. Some would say that the body and consciousness are different aspects of the same thing (a view closer to the Jewish Old Testament picture), others that they are interdependent but separate (a view closer to the Greek New

Testament picture). Whatever view we take we can all identify within our own experience a body and a consciousness. Our consciousness is aware of its surroundings by means of the senses, which emanate from the body. We have examined the limitations of these senses and seen that they cannot report to us everything that may be around, they can only report what they are tuned to reporting. Another source of information available to us is in the form of our genetic make up. Finally, we, as the human race, place a great deal of reliance on something that we could regard as intuition; for example, I know that I am not God.

As human, we find ourselves born into a reality that cannot sense or know God. We need God to reach to us. The Holy Spirit speaks to us and convicts us of our separateness from God, our sin, and offers us the solution that is Jesus: God became human, to live and die amongst us. His life was an example and his death our justification. His resurrection was God's propitiation. When we recognise and accept this, God brings about changes in our form.

We enter into a new relationship with (*en*) the Holy Spirit. This brings about changes in our make up. After our redemption, we become more aware of God. It is like having a new sense. It is not a sense that emanates from the body, but one that emanates from the Holy Spirit. We do not hear, see, touch, or smell God, but we have a channel of communication open to us that allows us to be aware of God, his presence, his prompting, his desires and it must be said, his offence. This awareness is not like our senses in that our senses are consistently available to us. This awareness comes and goes, it is sometimes strong and sometimes weak, but it is always there. It emanates from our relationship with God. It is like our senses in that it is part of us, we own it and can choose to use it or choose to ignore it.

Secondly, the Holy Spirit begins to equip us with abilities. These are given various names in the New Testament, the most well known being *charismata* which is often translated as "gifts". In this book I have tended to call these "giftings". What is common to all these giftings is that they enhance the ministry of the owner. I use the word "owner" quite deliberately as these giftings have been given to the individual who could therefore be seen as owning them. We have understood our senses to emanate from The Traveller's spacecraft, her body. We can understand these gifts as emanating from the Holy Spirit, although they are just as much The Traveller's as are her senses.

Some giftings are like senses in that they inform The Traveller about the world about her, not only that which is in her sense-reality, but also in total-reality. Some gifts allow her to gain a clearer appreciation of what is in the heart and mind of God. Like arms and legs, some gifts may be instruments that cause an effect, usually through prayer. Still others enhance existing abilities and gifts: ministry gifts that may be seen as natural may become spirit empowered through the help of Spirit given facilities. The Traveller will be able to make decisions about the way that she lives her life and the way that she relates to others using information from her spiritual giftings.

There is no end or limit to what the Spirit may and can do. Gifting is about as individual as individuality. Gifting can and will be used in an individual way.

The purpose of these giftings is to empower The Traveller to show Jesus, to equip her so that she may continue in her first life as an effective servant of God, to enter into a deeper and more understanding fellowship with him, and to become the praise of his glory.

Conclusion

In all four Gospels John the Baptist announces Jesus as the Baptiser in the Holy Spirit. The context of this description implies that it is not meant to describe part of Jesus' ministry but the whole. It is a proclamation of his purpose and it is the Holy Spirit's ministry to facilitate it.

The word "Baptism" refers to a process of change. Here, it starts when the Holy Spirit starts to convict an individual of his or her need for God. The Spirit then leads to the place of re-birth. The final stage is the equipping of the new Christian with spiritual gifts. This is the journey from sinner to servant. It occurs within the context of a relationship with God.

Salvation is part of this baptism. As such, it is a mistake to ask whether the baptism comes with, or is subsequent to salvation, as the salvation experience is a necessary part of the Baptism in the Spirit.[212] As part of this Baptism, spiritual gifts are given to the new

---

[212] The statement that says they "will" receive the Baptism is not a problem. This is like saying to a potential officer at the end of a period of training that he will receive his commission on a certain day or that a graduate will receive her degree on a certain day. The training, learning and preparation happened prior to the day. One would not say that a degree could be gained in a day.

Christian with and subsequent to their salvation. These gifts are many and varied.

To understand the Baptism in the Holy Spirit in this way changes the emphasis in evangelism. To complete the work, equal weight must be placed on the equipping of individuals with spiritual gifts as is given to the salvation message this is Christ's purpose.

Similarly, church structures must reflect that the role of the church is to promote, use and encourage the spiritual gifts within its community. This is not always so today. If it can be difficult for a junior minister to find opportunity to preach, it can be almost impossible for a young member of the laity.

This understanding changes the aspirations of ministers in the church. Rather than only ministering themselves, their task is to equip and train others in ministry in order to build up the body of Christ.

Churches should be factories, repair shops and facilitators of spiritual gifting. Undoubtedly, such unfettered possibilities allow many mistakes. The opportunities afforded by the correction of these serves to engage the gifting of the leaders. In such a church, you never know what is going to happen next!

This is Jesus' desire for his church. It is to be a body in which all live in fellowship *en* the Spirit, exercising all manner of gifting and abilities to the glory of God. It is for this purpose that he baptises us in the Holy Spirit; God seeks us, saves us, equips us and releases us to worship him through praise and service.

And when they were all together, he commanded them not to leave Jerusalem but to wait for *The Promise of the Father, "which,"* he said, *"you have heard of from me, because even as John baptized with water, you shall be baptized 'en' the Holy Spirit, not many days from now,"* Acts 1:4-5.